Organizational Change and the Third World

ORGANIZATIONAL CHANGE AND THE THIRD WORLD

Designs for the Twenty-First Century

ALLEN JEDLICKA

PRAEGER

New York
Westport, Connecticut
London

Library of Congress Cataloging-in-Publication Data

Jedlicka, Allen D.
  Organizational change and the Third World.

  Includes index.
    1. Economic development projects—Developing
countries—Management. 2. Economic development
projects—Developing countries—Citizen participation.
3. Organizational change—Developing countries.
4. Organization change.
I. Title.
HC59.72.E44J43   1987   658.4'06'091724   87–13252
ISBN 0–275–92317–7 (alk. paper)

Library of Congress Catalog Card Number: 87–13252
ISBN: 0–275–92317–7

First published in 1987

Praeger Publishers, One Madison Avenue, New York, NY 10010
A division of Greenwood Press, Inc.

Printed in the United States of America

∞

The paper used in this book complies with the
Permanent Paper Standard issued by the National
Information Standards Organization (Z39.48–1984).

10   9   8   7   6   5   4   3   2   1

Contents

List of Tables and Figures

Foreword

Organizational development has brought about significant increases in efficiency and productivity in the Third World, but, as a discipline, it traditionally has had one fundamental flaw. It does not address the most important component of any development program—the beneficiaries themselves. In this book, Allen Jedlicka asserts that these individuals play a critical role in organizational change, and his expertise provides practitioners with the tools to help bring them into that process.

I share Jedlicka's commitment to this process. To move into the twenty-first century, and to work toward real development in which the poor and disenfranchised gain power and autonomy over their lives, they must be part of the development process. Program beneficiaries must be involved in the planning, implementation, and evaluation of the very programs that have an impact on their lives. More importantly, beneficiaries must be prepared by development organizations for the day when they will be responsible for project management.

However, as most of us have found out in the field, creating meaningful mechanisms for the participation of project beneficiaries is not as simple as it would appear at first glance. Even the thought of "those" people having a say in project design, let alone management, puts most administrators and program managers into a cold sweat because it involves sharing power with an external group—people who are generally viewed paternalistically if not with contempt. Staff members do not recognize the value of their input. Talk of increasing participation in program implementation creates high levels of stress in the organization. Staff members begin to fear that if they do their jobs well and beneficiaries really do gain greater control over their environment, they will lose their jobs.

Jedlicka's book tackles this problem head on. He presents a strategy for bringing beneficiaries into the development process that, because it threatens the status quo of program staff, must include both attitudinal and institutional changes. He correctly asserts that the management style and systems of these organizations must change in order for this to happen. Before the beneficiaries are able to provide meaningful input into program management, program staff must understand and accept the importance and usefulness of joint decision making and appreciate the knowledge and expertise of their client groups. To prepare the organization for meaningful participation by the client group, Jedlicka presents a series of training sessions that challenges program staff to change their attitudes and helps sensitize them to the need and urgency of including their clients in the development process.

That clients can play an active and effective role has been repeatedly demonstrated in the field. Management Development International (MDI) has successfully used several of the techniques that Jedlicka discusses in this book. By creating appropriate procedures, support systems, field manuals, and training programs, an organization can develop a framework that allows for and facilitates the invaluable input of beneficiaries in the planning, implementation, and evaluation of development programs.

MDI has seen the tremendous impact that beneficiaries can have in program design through their participation in program evaluations. When we evaluate a development program, we hire a group of local residents as our "impact evaluation team"—as a complement to the technical team. Often, when conducting an impact evaluation, we must first refine and clarify a poorly defined program proposal. In such cases, with minimal training in program design, the impact evaluation team has always developed a program strategy superior to that prepared by central office technicians. After a day of training in evaluation and the use of the Logical Framework, a planning tool designed by the U.S. Agency for International Development, the local team is then responsible for the design of the survey instrument, carrying out interviews with community residents, tabulation of data, and presentation of a final report of principal conclusions to be included in the evaluation report. Consistently, this team provides hard-hitting, critical recommendations for improvements in program strategies because of their firsthand knowledge of program implementation.

Our experience from the field clearly demonstrates that, when communities have been given the opportunity and the logistical support to participate in program planning, program proposals are of higher quality. Objectives are clear and measurable. Strategies directly meet the needs of the client group, address their problems, and take advantage of their strengths. Because they are intimately aware of the local problems, restrictions, and resources, they are in the best position to plan cost-effective programs that take these into account. Jedlicka repeatedly stresses this, presenting a strong rationale for accepting and maximizing their input and providing practitioners with the means to facilitate that input. As the president of a firm that is constantly challenged to create mechanisms that provide the rural and urban poor with the means to participate meaningfully in the processes that affect their lives, I welcome this book and its practical applications.

Tonia Papke
Management Development International
New York City

Introduction

Some 30 years of concerted effort have gone into the development of the Third World, and there has been some success. India, which suffered severe economic problems in the 1960s, is now exporting wheat. China through its partial embrace of capitalism has also achieved agricultural self-sufficiency and now concentrates on improving its export capabilities.

At the same time, we are exposed to the specter of Africa—a whole continent where nothing seems to be working right. A common denominator in the economic development of all these countries is change. If carried out properly, change will truly introduce a new international economic order. But the caveat is that if the change process is not carried out properly we may have only seen the proverbial tip of the iceberg of economic calamity in the Third World.

This book focuses on that central concern of change and how one can facilitate the development of organizations that carry out the change process. As such, the book is concerned with five primary issues:

1. The management of the change process;
2. Cultural bias in the organizational change process;
3. The initiation of organizational change;
4. The development of Third World organizational change institutions; and
5. Methods of training people who will carry out the organizational change process.

Consequently, the book emphasizes a considerable reliance upon management technique in properly carrying out a change process. It has only been within the past decade that international change efforts have recognized the importance of good management in Third World development. It is hoped that this book will further clarify how improved management can be incorporated into the Third World development process.

The final point to be made is that not only is the Third World immersed in change, but so too is the First World. The evening news daily reminds us of how changing economic systems affect communities from Osaka to Des Moines. The First World, secure for 40 years from economic turmoil, is now entering a transition period and finding that solutions to problems are as intractable as they have been in the Third World.

The final resolution of the problem will be a truly world community that, barring a nuclear holocaust, will probably occur sometime in the second quarter of the twenty-first century. Our relations with the Third World will certainly be different than they are today, given that by 2050 it is anticipated that the world population will increase to 5 billion (96 percent of which will be in the Third

World). Hopefully, we will have the resources and sensitivity to carry out a process that will enable us to work together for mutual well-being.

There is going to be a major change process going through all the organizations and institutions the First World so cherishes. Such change will be necessary to meet the environment of the twenty-first century. Nobody says it is going to be easy, but everybody should recognize it will be mandatory.

This book thus serves as an introduction to a forthcoming book that will attempt to show how we can create a new order and a world development process, the organizational designs for a world community.

Organizational Change and the Third World

1

Overview: Development and Organizational Change in the Third World

> We're not stupid bastards. Those extension people are going to have to stop
> treating us like shit, and let us have a say in what is being done.
> Mexican Subsistence Farmer

INTRODUCTION

Throughout the Third World, a major component of today's development
problems is lack of involvement in the change process. Too often, people perceive change to be to their disadvantage, despite the fact that politicians say
conditions will improve if they just wait. The trickle-down theory is once again
proposed for development in the Third World. Like the Herblock cartoon about
the early days of the Reagan administration (a Republican elephant straddling
the U.S. economy in a large puddle), trickle down for world development has
too often amounted to the same thing. Mexican farmers have the ability to be
even more graphic in their assessment. One thing is certain in the remaining
days of the twentieth century and the early days of the twenty-first: change is
not going to occur quietly or neatly. It will not wait to be trickled down. It is
going to be noisy and full of a great deal of conflict. Conflict can be managed if
all people in the system have the right to participate on a more or less equal basis and to make meaningful contributions to that change process and if the managers of change programs acquire the behavioral skills to manage that conflict.

  If changes in the present system are going to occur, they will have to be
made conscientiously. The way organizations and the way people think and
behave within those organizations will have to be changed. That means, ultimately, some sort of training and management (that will benefit the people the
organization serves) will have to be developed or changed. But does this also
mean that the people who are served want and will participate in the process?

  The intent of this book is to show what can be done (and what is being done
in a number of organizations throughout the world) through organizational

change and to describe the kind of training required for that change process.

THE FIELD BACKGROUND

In earlier years, people talked about the turn of the century as the Third World Armageddon, the time when world starvation would be upon us and everything would go to hell. Ethiopia and the Sahel have shown us that, short of a couple of rock and roll concerts, we can live quite well with that reality. So what if 40 or 50 million people starve to death? That does not negate the need to try to change the situation. It merely recognizes that, like the old Ferlinghetti poem, world starvation is not so bad if it is not you who are starving. People will not be particularly upset, and the world will not come to an end. So one could logically suggest that it is futile to write books like this, which purport to show the way to improve world conditions. Is it not just as reasonable to ignore what is happening? The answer, of course, is in the news programs every night. Terrorism or the siege of the last colonial nation—South Africa—shows us that something must be done.

Much has been already attempted, but a major problem has been failure to manage the change process and train a staff that can effectively handle whatever change effort is at hand—be it birth control or farm extension. There are ways by which that can be done, and this book will focus on describing some of those ways. But before entering into the technical domain of how to go about effecting an organizational change process, some more explanation will be provided on the economic, political, and social reasons why conditions are as they now are.

ECONOMIC PITFALLS BEHIND EFFECTIVE ORGANIZATIONAL CHANGE

Although the ultimate motive of organizational change is to improve the lives of a specific group of people in a given country, the dynamics of the international economy ultimately and often very quickly offset any serious effort to improve living conditions.

As this book is being written, the spot market (cash) price for oil has dropped from $26 to $13 in four weeks, and analysts are predicting that it will ultimately drop below $10 before the summer is over. That means the oil-producing Third World countries will be seeing hard times.

Organizational change efforts, along with skilled, dedicated training personnel, require an investment of capital that can often be relatively expensive (there is no other way to get around it). With economic hard times, such efforts are typically the first to be cut; that is as true in the developed as in the developing countries. It is certainly true in the oil-producing, developing countries.

For example, only ten years ago, Mexico was viewed as one of those transition countries (on the verge of entering the lower levels of the developed countries). Basing most of their foreign exchange earnings on oil export and tourism, the Mexican government went into debt to the tune of $100 billion. Two things then happened: the price of oil dropped dramatically, and the 1985 earthquake disrupted the tourism industry. As a result, the country is bankrupt, and its creditors are stumbling on ways they might be able to restructure the debt load. So if one considers a Mexican desire to change its organizational structure to a mode more consistent with the approaching twenty-first century, you can see that there is not much of a capital base to do it with.

A classical sector in which to try organizational change in Mexico is the agencies that deal with agriculture. After all, they typically have some kind of extension staff, and some authorities take the view that changing that department alone (in an agricultural improvement organization) might be sufficient to make a major effect in the field.

Unfortunately, even if that scenario would work, there is a macroelement that in the end will probably make even that theoretically successful effort fail. That element is the reality that even success in field efforts (under the current types of agricultural production) may still mean failure in a macroeconomic sense.

A specific example is the distribution of land holdings in the Mexican agriculture system, as depicted in Table 1.1.[1]

Table 1.1.
Private Holdings: Mexican Agricultural Income by Farm Classification, 1980

Farm Type and Income	Percent of Farms	Percent of Value of Production
Subsistence ($0-$241)	78.6	5.4
Semicommercial ($241-$4,000)	18.5	23.3
Commercial ($4,001-$80,000+)	2.9	71.3

Note: These figures do not include ejidos; total number of farm units in survey is 997,324.

Focus on the subsistence sector that accounts for 78.6 percent of Mexican farms. Taking the maximum farm income of $241 as the mean (which it is not) and dividing it by the average Mexican rural family (of eight), you come to an average per capita income of $30. Unfortunately, the conventional wisdom that things are inexpensive in countries like Mexico just is not true. Clothes, electronics, gas, fuel, and basic foodstuffs (beans and corn) are all higher than in the United States. While the rural families can subsist on their own food production, they still have to buy clothes and charcoal to cook with (wood in the form of trees to cut down has long since disappeared). Charcoal for the average family, if they use it for boiling water as well, costs 75 cents U.S. a day. Multiply that by 365 days and you get $273 a year. You quickly realize that some of those meals are not hot and that most of the family's water is not boiled.

The major result, seen almost nightly on the evening news, is that those farmers, stuck in the subsistence category of agricultural production (well over half the population), have become displaced. They try to improve their economic plight by moving into the Mexican metropolitan areas where at least some social services (food subsidies, health care) are provided. Others begin the trek to the U.S. border in the hope of making it on the other side.

It is not that Mexico has not tried to stem the tide of displaced rural peoples. The success of such innovative agricultural programs as the Puebla Project (a case example to be referred to later in the book) started in the late 1960s and clearly showed that organizational change and consistent follow-through can create increased productivity in subsistence holdings. Yet the total end result matters little. Such innovative efforts, affecting what seems to be a large number of people (over 60,000 farmers in the Puebla Project), are a mere drop in the bucket when one considers the millions of rural people who are in the center of the problem and have been compelled to leave insufficient land holdings and uneconomic economies of scale which do not even provide agricultural subsistence.

Yet one must bear in mind that this depressing scenario of the Mexican agricultural sector describes a country where infrastructure is well developed and where (as stated earlier) it was felt to be an almost developed country only ten years ago. If you were to look at the rural scene of a country such as Guinea-Bissau where no infrastructure exists, one could come away really depressed.

One of the realities that must be faced in the organizational change approaches that will be presented in this book is that they cannot be implemented in a vacuum. One of the reasons why Mexico is in such a quagmire is that subsistence agriculture, as it exists now, either cannot be made profitable or, at best, can be made only minimally profitable. That is a problem the United States farmer has also recently experienced in a remarkably similar pattern to the Mexican farmer.[2] Significant efforts have been made to increase production, but a quote from a Mexican subsistence farmer who had been interviewed by an extension agent about why he did not use the agent's home organization technology (which theoretically would double his corn production) best summarizes the situation: "Doubling nothing is still nothing."[3] Something all developmentalists have to recognize is that even well-executed efforts can be hurt by world macroeconomics. The end result can be doubling nothing.

However, despite the terrible reality of Mexico and countries in the African Sahel, world statistics show that farm output in the Third World rose over 33 percent between 1971 and 1982. But overall statistics neglect showing that some of that production includes winter vegetables and fruit flown from the southern countries to Europe and the United States, that it includes canned tropical fruit shipped to the developed world, as well as range beef to be ground up for "Whopper" hamburgers. The fact is that over 60 percent of the world's population is either malnourished or starving, in ill health, uneducated, and living under conditions that most proper North American dogs would reject. The relentless population growth of the Third World continues and can lead inevitably to massive shortfalls in food distribution such as we have seen in Ethiopia.

The World Bank in 1985 has stated that the problem does not lie in food supply because in fact the world is oversupplied at the moment (an estimate for the end of 1986 is 250 million tons of stockpiled grain), but the real problem is the poverty of people who are unable to buy the food that is available (which is also true in the United States, especially among the 3 million homeless who now spend their winters on some heat exhaust grate in a large city).[4] But these facts have always been true. In Ethiopia during the famine of 1983, had the people money, they could have been able to buy food. The reasons for poverty are the most intractable of all because at the present time no one nation can necessarily control the factors that can remove poverty. We have already tested the route to resolving poverty through rapid industrialization of the Third World in the 1950s and 1960s. It largely failed since on a world market basis the product of such efforts could not compete effectively in a world market against the developed countries. While there have been regional success stories, as the developed world switches its productive system increasingly to a high-quality, low-cost, automated system, the ability of the Third World to compete will continue to fall behind. The one advantage such countries possess, abundant cheap labor, has little meaning in automated, high-technology, production systems.

The continuing reality for the majority of Third World people is that improvement of the standard of living and the elimination of poverty will still have to be through development of the rural areas by a combination of agricultural development, agribusiness, and small-scale industries. Given that industrialization has failed, and if we are to believe some of the futurists' theories that Third World countries should not duplicate the disruptions that a large-scale industrialization produces, then agricultural and rural development are the major alternatives to a relatively peaceful change process.

However, as has already been illustrated by the example of Mexico and the United States, agriculture throughout the world is undergoing a fundamental change. If developing countries rely upon agriculture as a primary means of improving the lives of people within the rural sectors, then an effort will have to be made to utilize new techniques and to change the organizations that supply those techniques so that their field effectiveness will improve. Instead of merely trying to make outdated products and techniques more efficient, new approaches and techniques will have to be presented. The organizations that present those techniques and approaches will have to do a better job than they have in the past.

The ultimate point to be made is that if there is not some integration of organizational change efforts with some kind of planning of what will be introduced to improve the economic reality of beneficiaries in the twenty-first century, then what one may end up with is highly effective organizations using a relevant, participative, behavioral technology with no place to go. With that concern in mind, it is important that economists and scientists be involved in the planning of the economic and technical objectives of any change effort. However, in this book the focus will be on the organizational means of carrying out those objectives—admittedly only one part of the total macroeconomic process.

ALTERNATIVES TO THE STATUS QUO

In the developed nations, farmers (especially in Europe and Japan—less so during the current economic dislocation in the United States) are a protected species. They receive price supports and other incentives to continue producing in their old, not necessarily all that efficient, way as a supply hedge against the future possibility of a war and a cut off of cheaper foodstuffs via the international market. In the developing countries, farmers more often are an exploited class receiving artificially lower prices for their products in order to benefit prices in the urban areas. They receive only minimal help in governmental price and infrastructure support that could improve their productivity. Governments need to recognize the effects of policy-induced failure. The failure of some African agricultural policies of focusing on big state farms (characterized by little productivity), is certainly one reason why several African countries are now in an agricultural production dilemma.

Moreover, we are facing a major revolution in agriculture that could lead to a pattern of agribusiness and rural small business development that does not follow the pattern of the developed world as it left subsistence agriculture for modernization.

For example, despite the current belief by some subsistence farmers that doubling nothing is still nothing, new agricultural technology could change things significantly. Consider how corn will be grown in the near future. Using nitrogen-fixing, perennial varieties, a farmer will only have to plant it once, and the plant will supply its own nitrogen. To provide jobs in the rural areas, the corn biomass can be used to make methanol in pilot-scale regional plants. This fuel, in turn, would be used to power farm equipment. From animal waste and some of the biomass, the farmer can produce methane gas for cooking and heating fuel. The biological digestion process does not waste the biomass, converting it instead into a nitrogen-enriched fertilizer that can be used to fertilize a truck garden and fish pond for the production of specific products for urban markets (this system already exists in Colombia and will be further discussed in Chapter 5). If a farmer desires to raise cattle on a limited basis, new varieties have been developed that are only the size of a St. Bernard yet have a meat-to-waste ratio considerably higher than today's standard cattle varieties. Farmers can feed this cattle largely on biomass treated with sulfuric acid, which they cook with methane generated on their farms. Furthermore, all of this can be done on a hectare of land. All these possibilities exist today and have been tested on a pilot study basis—the really exotic technologies such as amorphous crystallization, home electrical production, and home-based mini-manufacturing systems using robots are yet to come and will provide even more innovative opportunities in the future.

Alvin Toffler calls this the third wave, in which decentralized means of production will displace centralized means of production such as we now have in the developed countries.[5] The relevant point is that most production in the Third World is decentralized since the majority of the people are still living in rural settings. Using home-based systems of generating electricity and fuels eliminates the expense of a country developing the large, centralized infrastructure and delivery systems that exist in the developed countries. They theoretically would allow the Third World to bridge the gap between them and the developed nations within a few generations.

I believe that scenario is possible, provided the developed countries are willing to supply those technologies to the Third World, for one thing is certain: it is the First World countries that are developing them and will continue to do so.

The ultimate point to be made is that, if this scenario or part of this scenario is to take place, some rather radical high-level policy decisions will have to be made, and the commitment to follow through on those decisions will have to be maintained for the two or so generations it will take to implement them. Ironically, considering where it was only ten years ago, the most likely candidate for this kind of scenario being fully developed is China.

However, the other reality is that in order to carry out such an economic transformation (in some cases directly from subsistence to high-technology farming) the organizations that carry out those policies, by organizing and training recipients in how to use those new technologies, will have to have the behavioral skills to carry out the mission. Unless they are exceptional, their people will have to be trained in the methods of carrying out that mission by being highly effective managers and skilled extension agents. For without those skills, we can create new policies to infinity without any change. In the Third World, it is these people who are the equivalent of our astronauts, for their skill and bravery will have more impact upon the progress of their country's people (for better or worse) than any force within a particular country. As an example, given the public commitment to policy changes, in the Philippines of the Aquino government and a commitment to improve rural conditions through skilled extension people, it will be particularly interesting to see how soon policy actually affects organizations and their interactions with the people they serve during the coming years.

Organization change efforts have long been recognized as an important element in the process of development. It is just that it has frequently not been done well. The following section will discuss some of the efforts in earlier decades.

ORGANIZATIONAL CHANGE EFFORTS IN THE 1960s AND 1970s

When one looks at efforts to change the organizational structure and effectiveness of Third World change agencies, one immediately notes that much has been attempted in the 1960s and 1970s. The focus has been largely consistent, emphasizing that, if development is to succeed, attention will have to be paid to involving the people ultimately affected in the change effort.

The problem with most technology transfer programs . . . is that they ignore the needs and interest of the recipients. What is needed, therefore, is a more humanistic approach to management. In fact, much of the development model is even more appropriate for working with farmers in the third world then it is for working within large institutions in the West. Theory Y management directly addresses the fact that farmers are mature, adult, rational individuals . . . humanistic-democratic . . . management systems which by definition are willing to accept the conflict and uncertainty introduced by the clients' culture, are more suited to introducing change than are authoritarian systems that rely upon certainty, and submission by clients. Many administrators in third world nations (as well as the majority of corporations in first world countries) are not inclined to open, flexible procedures and relations. For this reason it becomes necessary to create new institutions and to train the managers of those institutions in human relations techniques. Training above all must affect those at the top for their priorities and influence largely shape organizational behavior. Without their conversion and commitment, training and changing the lower levels of the organization will probably result in little organizational change.[6]

This was the major thrust and message of an earlier book, *Organization for Rural Development,* written in a more optimistic decade where it seemed as though there might actually be a chance to raise consciousness, to green not only America, but the world, and finally to put a cap upon such elemental concerns as world hunger.

There have been prodigious changes in the last seven years. Consciousness raising in the United States has lowered its sights somewhat; some would even say it is dead. Furthermore, some people would say that organizational change has had its heyday and departed. The writings of Bennis, Beene, and Chin in the late 1960s influenced an entire generation of eager young researchers who tried to translate idealism and humanism into corporate change efforts.[7] For the greening of America was something that many thought could be extended to corporate America. For awhile, it looked like that could develop with a flush economy and flush corporation budgets. Organization change via organization development and management training became fairly common. Yet the bottom line was that the companies did not really want to change, that the acceptance of organizational change was born out of necessity because companies could not keep sufficient numbers of workers to do the job. So organizational change became a cynical way of trying to placate people sufficiently well to stay on the job, thus eliminating the expense of constantly retraining new people.

Unfortunately, as the 1960s became the 1970s and the 1970s became a depression, the greening of America went out the window, and automation and autocracy replaced humanism. Training and humanistic organizational change became unfashionable and probably will not return since many business executives frankly admit that they really do not need to bother with the expense of improving human relations on the job since the replacement labor force is large and cheap. Besides, most of it will be shortly replaced by automated systems. The position of U.S. workers increasingly looks like that of their Third World counterparts, characterized by pressures that produce lower wages as well as less concern for the person that earns the wage. Classical management and Frederick Taylor return to dominate management thinking because of tight economics and innovative computer systems.

An example of the backward progress in participation, humanism, and control of organizations in the United States is the new voice-activated checkout system in grocery stores, which also has a classical time and motion measurement device in it. The system automatically clocks the time it takes a checker to complete a specific task (for example, lifting a three-pound roast beef out of a cart and logging in the price). The computer then compares the time taken to an average estimated time and provides a printout to supervisors of how well the checker matched the ideal state of the company. A consistent failure to match average times results in dismissal. Equally loathsome is the increasing popularity of polygraph and drug tests to get or retain a job, as well as efforts to get constitutional changes to support those violations of the Bill of Rights. So while we have used the United States as an example of democracy and participation in action, the reality is that direct participation and control of the processes that affect individual life are also on the decrease. In many ways, the United States is as derelict in its duties as the Third World is in terms of allowing employees to control management systems. There is much that needs to be done in the United States, but that is the subject of another book.

Despite all the economic and technical reasons against it, the need for effective organizational change has never been higher in the Third World (if we want to believe that all economic enterprises are to benefit the people who participate in them and not merely to provide subsistence of mind and body). However, there are definite problems with serving the individual through management systems.

For in the final analysis, successful development cooperation will depend on the extent to which . . . purposes can be translated into effective mechanisms for dealing with problems over the long-term. Cooperation and funding of . . . programs should be based on need and insulated from transient, short-term political interest. But modern management techniques for business enterprises often translate poorly into the developmental area, where commitment to long-term objectives and dogged attention to detail are more likely to be successful than frequent change of personnel in a frustrating search for the "new approach" that will satisfy managers to the *detriment* of the ultimate subjects of the activities.[8]

The warning is made that improper management systems may penalize the people they are intended to serve.

Modern management techniques developed for business enterprises can, however, be translated properly into the Third World development arena provided the team that makes the modification has the skills to adjust for cultural differences. The major problem has always been that culturally insensitive people have far more often borne the responsibility of initiating the techniques and far more often have done a bad job of it. But that can be controlled and Chapter 3 will discuss specifically how this can be done. The following section will discuss some of the history behind cultural insensitivity in organizational change.

CULTURAL INSENSITIVITY IN ORGANIZATIONAL CHANGE

A common criticism of administrative reform of Third World organizations in the 1960s was a reliance upon techniques that were inappropriate for the cultural setting of the particular program. As stated by David Korten:

The U.S. public administration technologies which were exported were inappropriate both to the task of development and to the environment in which they were to be used. The emphasis on rules, procedures, formal structures, position classifications, PPBS, and formal organizational specifications was better suited to system improvement within well institutionalized socio-political systems than to the need of the third world nations for system development. Furthermore, these tools and techniques were not adequate for establishing organizations that would produce new outputs, stimulate new forms of behavior in their environment, and which would continue to be innovative over time.[9]

As a young Peace Corps volunteer in the 1960s, I can testify to some of the absurdities that this kind of management led to. We were expected to give semiannual reports to the substitute planning section of the State Department.

In fact, rather precise estimates were required concerning how many people we had influenced about the U.S. way of life and how many people we had influenced who were now in support of the United States. Several of us, being rather naive, wrote letters to various bureaucrats informing them of the absurdity of such a procedure, only to be informed that we were not following procedures and that a formal reprimand (horrors) had been placed in our files.

Furthermore, as Korten continues to note:

The separation of planning and implementation left the planners far removed from reality and generated in some a sense of omnipotence and a disdain for the "lesser folk" who were simply to follow their dictates. The separation also failed to recognize that the principal benefit of planning is not always the plan itself, but the anticipatory and participatory experience gained from involvement in the planning process.[10]

The participatory process is the primary element in organizational change and will be presented in detail in Chapter 2.

Furthermore, a tragedy is that too much of the training offered by international agencies still focuses upon this misled reliance upon top-downward, bureaucratic management that neglects the input of the crucial element in development efforts—the people to be served by a program. One only has to look at the outlines of many contemporary training programs for foreign personnel to see that much of the 1960s format still exists. Standing proud are the ubiquitous courses in Program Evaluation and Review Technique (PERT), cost-benefit analysis, PPBS, and organizational procedure. What you tend to see little of is training on how to change central administration's views toward beneficiaries, how to involve clients in the decision-making process, and how to implement change as a mutually shared program between organization bureaucrats and the people affected by the central organization (in fairness, some countries would not allow people to be trained in such revolutionary tactics). But if we are to establish the twenty-first century as the beginning of a new world order, then we must begin to act seriously upon the involvement of people who are to be changed and must change the management processes that affect people.

One thing that can be said about the twentieth century is that as it closes, whether planned or not, the developed world has effectively disrupted every society. As a result, the discipline or art of anthropology no longer exists—the primitives are gone. What the developed countries obviously have done is a poor job of integrating all those societies (since we, for the most part, do not kill them off as we did in the nineteenth century) into the world economic mainstream. Greed and rivalry among nations have obviously played some role in the slowness of such integration. While internal control devices like PPBS and rigid bureaucratic procedure that do not account for differences in behavior may be effective within a bureaucracy, they do not work so well when one is trying to convince the Yanamomo Indians to adopt a high-lyzine corn seed. Someone who understands the "bureaucracy," if you will, of that culture is needed. To carry out that developmental process, we will need administrators who understand behavioral-organizational technology and who will have the cultural sensitivity needed to carry out such a role successfully.

As recently as 1979, it could still be said by too many authorities in the field that the use of behavioral-organizational technologies needed in the management process of development had not been given much attention by those concerned with the planning and implementation processes. Consequently, as Korten points out, what was largely not created (which could have been executed through the proper use of behavioral-organizational technology) was the ability to organize the poor for participation in making policy decisions and for developing organizations capable of adapting rapidly (because of the behavioral training of its administrator) to changing local conditions.[11] That must be changed in creating designs for the twenty-first century.

In the improper use of management technique in Third World countries, there is a parallel to the military where, as Gwynne Dyer states, "the temptation to believe that all the human imponderables of combat can be reduced to neat equations was especially strong in the United States during the Vietnam War and exalted the role of the manager and planner over that of the traditional fighting commander." There was the overoptimistic belief that correct managerial techniques and appropriate technology will solve anything. "Computer technology carefully biasing the data that go into it can furthermore assure analysts that a good job is being done when in fact it isn't."[12]

In Third World development, there is also a limit as to how far formal management and planning can carry you. Ultimately, there are frontline people (fighting commanders for rural development?) who effectively use behavioral technology and who add the human element that makes a success of all the management, planning, and training that the organization provides its people. Like a battle, rural development is a situation where change agents have many variables they cannot control. Because of the limitations of control, there are many things affecting their decision-making process that they simply do not know. Consequently, if the central organization can control, at least, the training of representatives so that their analysis of the situation is at least consistent, the organization stands a better chance of success in its efforts to improve the life of the beneficiaries. If that training includes an ability to organize beneficiaries into the participation of that process, so much the better. But the key is the field worker, not irrelevant or biased managerial technique and assessment. In support, Korten states that:

Organization and management systems usually have been treated mechanistically, and not considered issues of real substance, those intellectuals who addressed development issues considered the making of policy to be the real issue worthy of their attention and thus, the concentration was on the quantitative-analytic technologies as the means for getting rationality into the key development decisions, these technologies were gradually reduced into readily transferable decision-making and planning methodologies, thereby greatly facilitating their dissemination.[13]

We might add that such dissemination largely avoided the interaction of the beneficiary base. A focus, then, of this book will be to present ways by which behavioral-organizational technologies can be applied to fill the major void of client participation that has been too characteristic of the last two decades of developmental efforts. The well-trained manager and the beneficiaries play the central roles, not the specific management technique.

Finally, one must remember that the objective of Third World development is to benefit the have-nots, and hopefully a little faster than a trickle down (which too often translates into the elites metaphorically urinating upon the nonelites). That is undoubtedly a hopeless view of reality because, as numerous bureaucrats have told me in numerous international development agencies, development has nothing to do with actually helping people. It exists as a pointless effort by the elites in the hope that they may shorten their tenure in purgatory by showing how they tried (to no avail) and thus advance their positions within the organization. Yet someday, sooner or later, change organizations have to be concerned with helping people, and when that day arrives, fortunately, the techniques exist to change that cynical reality. Many of the international development agencies in existence today may become irrelevant.

ON THE POLITICAL NATURE OF BENEFICIARY PARTICIPATION

In order not to appear hopelessly naive when talking about the involvement and participation of client groups in development, a short discourse on the nature of the political process and its effect on participation is relevant.

Undoubtedly the biggest impediment to the use of participation in development is the political structure of the country. If a strongly autocratic power is in force, which does not wish to support participative approaches, then those that advocate and implement such efforts are probably facing some risk. Three countries that outstandingly epitomize this are Guatemala, El Salvador, and the Philippines.

Developmentalists obviously cheer the election of the new civilian Guatemalan president Vinicio Cerzezo (after 30 years of military control), yet he must continue to walk a tightrope in the coming years between appeasing the military and advancing his own desires for greater freedom and involvement of local people in the decision-making process. He knows he must go cautiously so that the military will not quickly overthrow him, yet not so slowly so that the citizenry becomes further disenchanted and behaves in a way that will invite the army to take over. But he recognizes that the tightrope must be walked if the

Guatemalan economy is to revive. As shown in an interview in the television program "60 Minutes," the man sleeps lightly with a Uzi submachine gun on the night table. President Duarte, in El Salvador, is in a similar position.

If one were to look at the survivability of the men and women who try to organize and promote participation among the urban and rural poor, you find that their lifespans (once they become effective in that capacity) are too often short—there is little chivalry, for women fare no better. The situation in the Philippines during the Marcos regime indicated a pattern of assassination of reformers for over 20 years. Of course, this scenario is depressingly repeated in other countries in Africa, Asia, and South America.

Consequently, much of what follows in this book may never be applied in certain countries—at least in the short run. The simple reality is that allowing participation by beneficiaries in the change process inevitably means the generation of conflict and, to some extent, less control of the power base by the elites as integrated people become the power base and take charge of their lives. That reality is as true for union leaders in the United States, who really do not want to see the rise of participation in company decision making, since it diminishes the need for them, as it is for a military government in Central America. The difference is we do not kill the reformers, although we have in other decades. Such a reality does not mean that there is little worth in the approach; it merely means that in some areas of the world we will have to wait a little longer. Hopefully, in its own small way, this book will contribute to expediting that process. I still firmly believe in the Bennis view that democracy is inevitable.[14]

FIRST WORLD AND THIRD WORLD CHANGE INTERACTIONS

A reality in any major effort to change the behavior of Third World countries is the interplay between the major world powers (and some of the lesser world powers) with Third World governments. Obviously, we can pressure smaller governments to behave in the way that we think is proper—toward increasing democracy and satisfying basic human needs. For example, the U.S. Agency for International Development (AID) must make a preliminary assessment of the planning efforts of new projects. It is now required that the potential impact of satisfying the basic needs of the recipient community must be specifically addressed. This is a worthwhile effort even if, after the bureaucrats finish their assessment, it is sometimes hard to determine whether those needs have really been described (there exists, in certain documents, an almost incomprehensible jargon for describing such elemental concerns that go beyond the basics of people gotta eat, people gonna need housing, etc.). Increasingly, statements that greater participation of the potential beneficiaries is needed are being made in project assessments—a step in the right direction. But too often the political component of any international effort undermines those good intentions by subverting the potential for a significant change for the beneficiaries in a particular regime of a given country. The case of Marcos, as briefly touched upon earlier, is a relevant case.

For the last five years, rural development efforts in the Philippines, sponsored by the United States, have focused on many of the ideas expressed in this chapter, namely, that participants should be involved in the decision-making process, that involvement if not control of regional political forces should be directed to local people, and that target concerns should be the satisfaction of basic human needs. There has, of course, always been suspicion that the development or accomplishment of such objectives was never actually carried out because of the reputation of the Marcos regime—which at best can be described as not good. Continued exposure by the Aquino government confirms that suspicion.

The investment in the Philippines occurred because too many U.S. politicians spoke of Marcos as a "friend" of the United States. As Meg Greenfield put it, Marcos's "failure raises in the most interesting way questions about the widely accepted premise that strongman governments, while exacting a price in democratic freedoms, may be necessary to protect third world countries from the designs of predatory communism." Consequently, "Marcos and Co. have plundered their own country so that, far from being a showcase of the social and economic benefits that can flow from close association with the United States, the Philippines has become a metaphor for economic and social degradation."[15] The result of supporting a corrupt strongman in this case has been detrimental to both the health of the average Philippino and the reputation of the United States as being a country concerned with the improvement of the human condition. Only a cynic would say that U.S. support of such a morass as the Marcos regime could have been influenced by the fact that Subic Bay is used as a source of cheap Philippino labor to repair naval ships and that Clarke Air Force Base serves as a backup for a Pacific line of defense, should world events become less peaceful.

Certainly, this is only one more example of how expediency or just simple arrogance (Somoza and Nicaragua was another recent example) affects the chances of making an effective change in the world condition for poor people. In the end, it wastes far too many resources and all too often too many lives. Obviously, there will be more of this occurring. Members of the foreign services who establish these relationships, despite the patina of being on top of things, are not all that bright and, despite their autocratic manner, too often have no real idea of what is going on.

The situation may sound rather hopeless, but in actuality it is not. Paraphrasing Gwynne Dyer, humanity has spent 10,000 years engaged in the great experiment of civilization (a short second in the roughly 2 million years that humans and protohumans have been around) in which war and injustice to many have been a fact of life.[16] Such conditions, of course, still exist, but at least (due in large part to the potential Armageddon of nuclear weapons) we have reached the point where we are openly talking about and attempting to help others throughout the world (even if we are not all that effective). In the context of Third World development, look how far we have come in only a hundred years. A century ago, the solution for helping was to accept the responsibility of "the white man's burden" and meanwhile use the new innovation of the machine gun and improved artillery to quell any desire to get the white man out of what is the now Third World. (The average white man, after all, was not doing much better himself in the industrial sweatshops of his home country, although his expressions of discontent were not typically treated with machine gun therapy.)

By the end of the next hundred years (if we have not blown ourselves up), the problem will be solved, because the Third World will form its own cartel, if necessary, to ensure that the First World improve its condition. But the Group of 77, as a leader of that cartel (at the moment a relatively ineffective force in the U.N. with its demands upon the technostructure of the First World), is going about things all wrong. It should strike at the heart of the business community. Given that the hope of many business executives is to expand sales and operations in the Third World, a better approach to get what a country wants is to refuse to buy the products of the industrial First World. Do that and let the power of the international business lobby go to work on helping the Third World and itself. One only has to look at South Africa to get a primitive idea of how that might work, for it is business leaders who are now saying that racial conflict is bad and that it is time to take a second look at present policy and future profits.

Despite all this, I am basically optimistic that the behavioral technology I believe in (which will be discussed in this text) will ultimately be applied and will be utilized on a wide scale to create organizational change in both the Third and First Worlds. For those of us who believe in these approaches and have worked so long on them, the problem is that we will probably never see them come to complete fruition in our lifetimes. But with a little luck, we may be able to see a trend in that direction. It is certainly worth continued work.

For in reality we really have no choice. And in this regard, I speak also of the common worker in First World countries. Organizational change will be as much a fact of life in the twenty-first century for such workers as it is for the citizens of the Third World. There can be no other choice for the industrial organization and interpersonal relationships of the twentieth century cannot be effectively utilized in the changing world of the twenty-first century. The only effective change mechanism will be greater participation, and more underlying acceptance by those who have the power, be they department heads in business schools or bureaucrats in Third World change agencies. We must acknowledge that the people who count are reasonably mature and intelligent people who must be treated as such and that participation is inevitable.

In the interim, to try to control the political problems of working with regimes such as Marcos's, a workable solution might be to form an international effort to let agencies such as CARE, which are specifically nonpolitical in nature and autonomous from control of their own home county governments, play a larger role in the development of the Third World.

This is an idea that is increasingly presented in the United States, particularly by officials from the Reagan administration. For example, Dennis Avery, senior agricultural analyst at the State Department, asserts that in solving the associated problems of development such as better public health services, improved technology, and greater economic opportunities, the process will involve far-reaching changes in institutions. He then discusses the shortsighted policy failures of many governments and finally suggests

that voluntary organizations, with their ability to patrol constantly in remote corners of society, mobilize quick responses to local problems and deal delicately with individual problems, will assume vital importance in overcoming the remaining problems of hunger and poverty that still threaten significant numbers of the world's citizens.[17]

One always suspects, given the nature of the Reagan administration, that the motive behind such statements is to find yet another way to get something done without paying the bill. Yet there is much value to that statement, and a final argument toward utilizing that voluntary force not only for Third World development but for world development will be presented in the final chapter.

SUMMARY

It is not particularly new for most people to be told that the world is currently in a state of crisis and that millions of people are being hurt. Unfortunately, at this time a vast majority of our nation's students have little understanding of the current world situation nor any real desire to do anything about it. It makes one wonder what will happen when that generation effectively comes to power somewhere around 2025 (one characteristic of the yuppie generation is a decided lack of concern about the world other than their own). But maturity may change even them.

In addition to resolving the problems of the Third World, we also have another world experiment taking place. In the Soviet Union, Mikhail Gorbachev's publicized reform efforts clearly show that the best way to go about achieving effective change is through democratic processes. The trend throughout the world is to reject socialist-based approaches and move toward democratic efforts for economic development. Even Gorbachev has recognized that and is initiating policy changes. The changeover to democratic government in the Philippines and Latin America (one might also consider the changes in

China to be a democratic reform) all point to the fact that the socialist model does not work. George Will states, "The Soviet Union has passed its apogee of its doomed attempt to keep pace with the West. As the world becomes more complicated, it requires of societies fluidity, adaptability, and other prodigees of freedom."[18] It also illustrates that a highly centralized, nonparticipative system just does not work and indicates clearly to the leaders of the Third World that they will have to create the *policies* that will unleash the forces of participation and freedom if they are to develop their countries successfully. Recognizing and acting upon that reality (and recognizing the political difficulties of carrying this out in many Third World countries), there is a great deal that can be done through the use of existing behavioral and management technology. We can effectively create organizational changes and designs for the twenty-first century. This book, in its modest way, offers suggestions by which those designs can be created.

NOTES

1. The source of Table 1.1 is the Mexican agricultural department report, Quinto Censo Agricola, Ganadero, y Forrestal, for the year 1980—the latest Mexican report on agricultural holdings.

2. One irony about this is that the U.S. farmer, while having a considerably larger capital base, is in the same position of being essentially a subsistence farmer. To illustrate this point, focus on the category $5,000 to $9,999 of annual sales in Table 1.2.

Table 1.2
U.S. Farm Characteristics by Sales Class

	Thousands of farms	Gross farm income*	Net farm income*	Net family income per farm	Net worth per farm**
		(billions of dollars)		(dollars)	(dollars)
Farms with annual sales of:					
$500,000 and above	25	45.6	14.3	597,900	2,650,300
$200,000-499,999	87	29.5	4.7	67,200	1,274,900
$100,000-199,999	186	30.4	3.7	30,900	821,500
$100,000 and above	298	105.5	22.7	89,100	1,107,300
$40,000-99,999	393	31.3	2.2	16,200	482,400
$20,000-39,999	273	10.5	0.1	13,400	290,500
$10,000-19,999	281	6.0	-0.2	16,500	176,500
$5,000-9,999	331	4.4	-0.3	18,300	116,800
Less than $5,000	824	6.3	-0.5	19,500	70,000
Less than $39,999	1,709	27.2	-0.9	17,800	131,800
All farms	2,400	164.0	23.9	26,400	310,300

*Before inventory adjustment.
**As of January 1, 1983.
Source: U.S. Department of Agriculture, *Economic Indicators of the Farm Sector*, 1982.

Of special note is the seeming paradox that net family income per farm reaches a low of $13,400 for farms with annual sales of $20,000 to $39,999 and then actually increases as the annual sales figure decreases. This is not a statistical aberration but rather reflects the fact that the 824,000 "farm families" in the less than $5,000 annual sales category, for example, also receive a second nonfarm income. The availability of nonfarm income is an important source of both capital to expand the size of the operation and income for consumption purposes. When nonfarm employment is unavailable, farm operations of this size are not economically viable, and analogous to the Third World. Such farmers, in essence, are subsistence farmers since they have an income putting them into the poverty category for the United States.

In the United States, 1.7 million of the nation's 2.4 million farms have annual sales of less than $40,000. This group, which comprises about 71 percent of U.S. farms, produces only 16.6 percent of gross farm returns and actually experienced losses on their operations. On the other hand, the 298,000 units with sales in excess of $100,000 produced 64.3 percent of the farm sector's gross income and earned 95 percent of net farm income.

That figure of 71 percent in the subsistence sector is amazingly close to the Mexican figure of 78 percent and indicates that the Third World is not the only region of the world where governments have failed large numbers of its people. The U.S. Department of Agriculture is also in need of some dramatic organizational changes.

3. Field notes from the author's summer follow-up research in Huejotzingo, Mexico, July 1976.

4. Dennis Avery, "A Little Understood Reality: Hunger Is Not the Problem," *Des Moines Register,* March 23, 1986.

5. Alvin Toffler, *The Third Wave* (New York: William Morrow, 1980).

6. Allen Jedlicka, *Organization for Rural Development* (New York: Praeger, 1977), p. 37.

7. Warren Bennis, *Changing Organizations* (New York: McGraw-Hill, 1966).

8. Michael Dow, "Science, Technology, and African Famine," *BOSTID Developments* 5 (1985):16-19.

9. David Korten, *Population and Social Development Management* (Caracas, Venezuela: Instituto de Estudios Superiores de Administracion, 1979), p. 22.

10. Ibid., p. 22.

11. Ibid., p. 11.

12. Gwynne Dyer, *War* (New York: Crown, 1985), p. 139.

13. Korten, *Population and Social Development Management,* p. 22.

14. Bennis, *Changing Organizations.*

15. Meg Greenfield, "An Asian Notebook," *Newsweek,* February 10, 1986, p. 83.

16. Ibid.

17. Avery, "Hunger Is Not the Problem," p. 2C.

18. George Will, "Consumers Should Deal the Soviet System," reprinted in the *Des Moines Register,* March 23, 1986, p. 2C.

2

Management of the Change Process— Behavioral Technology

> We know almost nothing about the special capacities of the group. We all recognize that there are problems which can't be solved by an individual— not only because of limitations of time and energy, but because the individual, no matter how extraordinary, can't master all the aspects, can't think thoughts big enough.
>
> B. F. Skinner
> *Walden II*

INTRODUCTION

Times have changed since *Walden II* was written in 1948, and, in fact, we now know a great deal about the special qualities of the group. We know that individuals will accept greater risk-taking behavior in the context of the group interaction process. We know that groups are capable of performing very complex decision analyses in the context of facilitated, well-maintained, group dynamics. And we know that the group process typically produces a better solution to complex problems in part because of the synergistic effect of group interaction. But without the development or promotion of participation within, among, and outside the change organization, none of these benefits will arise, for effective group development cannot take place in an autocratic vacuum. It must be nurtured with the help of administrators who understand its importance and who are capable of developing, facilitating, and sustaining that process. A later section of this chapter presents the issue of women as being natural-born nurturers and facilitators and thus superior change agents. For it may very well be that a major problem with development is that its domination by men has led to reliance upon autocracy and inflexibility—attributes that in today's world of change can no longer be effective.

THE ROLE OF PARTICIPATION AND GROUP DEVELOPMENT IN ORGANIZATIONAL CHANGE

A major thesis in an earlier book by the author was that reliance upon a top-downward management structure, with a strong emphasis on authoritarian rather than group control, will not be able to provide a flexible enough response to changing conditions within the organization.

Warren Bennis, in particular, at least during the late 1960s when U.S. universities were very involved in the concept of "the greening of America," believed that rapid change, the condition of the world in the late twentieth century, required:

1. Full and free communication, regardless of rank and power.
2. A reliance on consensus rather than coercion to resolve conflict.
3. An atmosphere that permits and even encourages emotional expression as well as task-oriented acts.
4. A basically human bias, one that accepts the inevitability of conflict between the organization and the individual but is willing to cope with and mediate this conflict on rational grounds.[1]

Unfortunately, the implementation and practice of such beliefs, at least in the developed world of the United States, have not followed through. If anything, the situation has backslided more toward the management style of the late nineteenth century where policy dictates procedure and the common worker toes the line or gets out (more often not voluntarily). Perhaps surprisingly to laypersons, the increasing home of such organizational behavior in the United States is the university, where studies indicate that the most common faculty complaint is the autocratic behavior of university administration. This is even more disappointing to note because the university, theoretically a bastion for more humanitarian thought and the repository of humanistic training for future generations, cannot itself act in a reasonably participative manner. The situation is similar in the nation's industries, although in certain sectors such as the "silicon valley" microelectronics industries, a strong reliance on individual freedom and nonautocratic administrative behavior has made those companies able to operate more or less in the manner prescribed earlier by Bennis.

In a nineteenth century organization, such as a U.S. university, problem diagnosis in making an organizational change effort would be done solely by the people at the top of the organization. As stated in Chapter 1, these people have to be coopted, changed, and committed to the idea of totally changing the organization. But in a participative organization, the classic idea of top-downward organizational structure has to be changed. That is the classical pyramid view that people at the top are the ones who are in the best position to solve problems

Change Involving everyone

that affect the rest of the members of the organization, as illustrated in Figure 2.1.

Figure 2.1
Classical nineteenth century model of traditional administrative structure.

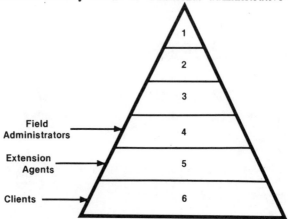

Source: Allen Jedlicka, *Organization for Rural Development* (New York: Praeger, 1977). Reprinted by permission of the publisher.

In contrast, in a participative, organizational environment, people at the bottom will more likely possess the information that is really needed to make effective organizational changes. In diagnosing organizational problems in such an organization, one would accept the view that people in the lowest levels would need to play a role in diagnosing that problem, and one would explicitly assume that the people at the top are in the worst position to analyze organizational problems. Furthermore, in a participative environment, small work groups would be utilized in making that diagnosis (the specific nature of work groups will be presented in a later section of the chapter).

Accepting the view that work groups are an effective mode of energizing the synergistic effect of different individuals, small work groups can be an effective means of diagnosing problems. There is a variety of evidence to support that view. For example, in the writer's organizational design courses, unskilled students are trained via a variety of exercises to become a cohesive work unit skilled in diagnosing problems in organizational settings they have never experienced before. Yet in six weeks they become experts, in the organizational environment they study, in applying human relations approaches to people-based problems within the organization. Another more directly related example was a management training program in the Beni section of Bolivia directed by Tonia Papke of Management International.[2]

The thrust of the problem-solving effort in this project was that clients, in this case Indian farmers, were brought directly into a small group to diagnose management organizational problems and then allowed to contribute jointly to the development of a program to address these problems. In the hands of a skilled specialist, there is really no reason why even illiterate client participants cannot contribute to the development of a training program and even specific training exercises. It is a fallacy that only highly trained specialists are capable of creating training programs or organizational changes. It is not exactly the same as brain surgery. Any sensitive person who has his/her own world experience in dealing with other humans has a rich bank of personal experience that can be integrated into the development of a training program and organizational change efforts.

Another reason for emphasizing the use and development of groups in organizational change efforts is that groups have both a cost and effectiveness advantage. When groups are effectively developed, more people can be served by a smaller staff, which consequently reduces the cost of change.

CURRENT USES OF GROUPS IN ORGANIZATIONAL CHANGE

One Third World country that has been particularly effective in training, co-ordinating, and using groups is China, which uses groups, throughout the country, as both a peer-pressure enforcement and extension service device.

The Chinese system in many ways is not unlike the ancient Inca system of control where district populations were subdivided into factors of ten until finally village-level groups of ten people were "facilitated" by an official of the state government. Even with the crude communication devices of the fourteenth century, it was possible for the administrative head, the Inca, to get essentially immediate information about anybody in the empire.

The disadvantage of the Inca system, from a humanistic standpoint, was that such immediate, intimate knowledge of the citizens made it extremely simple to control the population, which is essentially what happened. Citizens who violated the strict codes of the empire were quickly discovered and punished. Freedom of speech was largely limited to praise of the system and the Inca who dominated it. With today's improved communications, that sort of control is even easier to establish.

The Chinese birth control system is a modern example that parallels the ancient Inca system. To begin with, Chinese objectives in controlling birth control are based on a very probable twenty-first century scenario, namely, that without a significant and radical program to curtail reproduction, mass starvation throughout the country could be reestablished early in the century. The current policy of restricting each family to one child will sufficiently reduce an increase in population to prevent famine. Therefore, the government rapidly created the policy of only one child per family as the national norm. The means of doing this has been through the use of the small group as a control and diffusion device, specifically, groups that are linked in a two-way communication mode.

In an earlier book, I strongly advocated the development of a Likert linking-pin approach as an organizational means of getting Third World change agency clients to become actively involved in the change and development process. That approach will be briefly summarized here because it is relevant to the Chinese example. Under the linking-pin approach, managers are trained to think of themselves as members of overlapping circles of authority and responsibility. Instead of having an autocratic top-downward management system in which the bottom layers of the organization have no say in the direction of the organization, the overlapping layers of responsibility are thought of as devices whereby the lowest level can transmit its concerns and ideas to the highest level[3] (see Figure 2.2).

Figure 2.2
The Likert Linking-Pin Structure of a Change Organization

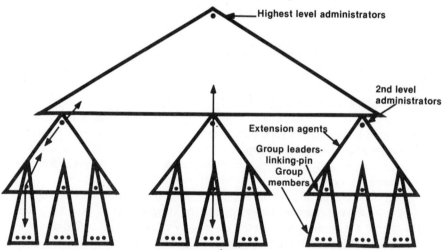

Source: Allen Jedlicka, *Organization for Rural Development* (New York: Praeger, 1977). Reprinted by permission of the publisher.

The lowest level is organized into small groups using all the benefits of small group dynamics to involve members and obtain their input. The decision-making results from the group are then transmitted through the levels to the highest administrative levels of the organization. Rensis Likert makes the argument, and supports it with some field studies, that such a structure will promote change and the active involvement and commitment of members in the process. Unfortunately, that is all based on the assumption that the highest levels of management support that philosophy. In fact, more recent evidence shows that such a structure can actually be even more controlling and autocratic. The issue is abuse of the technique, not the technique per se.

Specifically, recent investigations of Japanese automobile companies, which use a similar structure involving small work groups called quality circles (as the lowest level for the worker input source), provide an example of how a participative, group approach can be used for autocratic control. Much has been said about the use of quality circles as an example of industrial democracy in action, but more recent evidence seems to suggest that quality circles can be used as an environment where the group leader of the circle is the company informer, who reports back to higher levels of management those workers who are not singing the company line (and in fact may be openly criticizing it). Such evidence ultimately is used for the dismissal of the employee.

The tragedy of such industrial practices is not only the perversion of the democratic purposes behind the development of the quality circle, small group approach, but the additional use of the technique as an autocratic control device. People soon learn in the circles to restrict their comments. In the long run, such behavior (and the basic lack of trust) will hurt productivity because small groups cannot function effectively in such an environment.

This capacity for evil exists in strongly democratic structures because one of the essentials in their development is training and developing openness and trustworthiness among group members. If people are trained to be trusting, and become committed to these lofty ideas, then it becomes relatively easy for a manipulative group member to betray what is expressed in such meetings. Unfortunately, the close contact of quality circle members allows the manipulative participant to acquire extensive information that can be used against specific group members. It is an unfortunate paradox that democratic methods can be used for autocracy.

Returning to the earlier description of Inca society, the original intent of small-group development (basically democratic methods) was not for the benefit of the participant but for control by the state. The Peruvians long beat the Japanese in distorting good ideas. Today, organizational structures can be utilized either for a very tight autocratic control or a very open democratic industrial society. It largely depends upon the philosophic orientation of the highest levels of management, which dictate the nature of organizational procedure.

The issue of training and organizational change, in the end, thus becomes an issue of philosophical choice. Democratic structures (combined with other applied behavioral science techniques such as operant conditioning, i.e., the use of positive reinforcement by managers in supervising subordinates) can be highly efficient tools for either democracy or autocracy. Ultimately, top management and governmental policy makers will decide how behavioral technology will be used.

THE USE OF ORGANIZATIONAL CHANGE IN CHINA

The discussion above has diverged rather extensively from the subject of Chinese birth control programs, but it is totally relevant to the Chinese example. The birth control program follows a Likert structure right to the point of small-group development where the political officer/blockmother plays the part of the linking-pin to higher orders of authority. The blockmother has many applied behavioral tools at her disposal. She can operant condition the deviant mother (who wants more than one child) with rewards of scholarships for the one child, through additional rations from the state and through public rewards of praise and recognition. She can also negatively condition the mother by with-holding extra rations or threatening her with state indoctrination policies, such as less pay and additional negative reinforcement if she has the extra child. Combined with all of this is the additional peer pressure of the mother's block group, which can treat her as the group deviant and put even more pressure upon the mother to conform to the wishes of the state as represented by the linking-pin, block mother.

So there is an operational dilemma in introducing democratic-group-based organizational change efforts in environments that have a political background component. As stated before, there is a capacity for evil or, at least, nondemocratic consequences. On the one hand, the Chinese model has a capacity for greater efficiency, because when push comes to shove the state can "motivate" the reluctant participant by imposing the state's decision, that is, making the unwilling mother who cannot be convinced by the democratic pressures of the group to submit to a state decision such as nonvoluntary abortion. In terms of organizational change and human relations theory, this is a nonproductive approach that will make it difficult for the group member to believe in the organization in the long run. One can predict that it will continue to cause the Chinese government some trouble, particularly as the country becomes more affluent.

On the other hand, for most Third World countries, we can assume that the ultimate power of the state in making the individual's choice for them will not be enforced. Thus, the skill of the change agency in training linking-pins and extension staff who can convince (without power to enforce) becomes primary. The trick is to get the political support to recruit and train these people and control these imperatives for a changing world.

This may be more an issue for Western planners than it is for the people affected since the argument may be that hungry stomachs do not care what kind of idealism fills them or whether small group organization is used for autocratic purposes. Politically that may be true, but political idealism in the Third World can affect full bellies rather surprisingly and in a differential manner in the long run. Belly filling in Ethiopia seemed primarily focused upon the party faithful in the urban areas. In South Africa blacks who wish to go along with apartheid are similarly belly-filled, and so on and so on, country by country.

Applied behavioral science is a two-edged sword, and the jury is not yet in on whether techniques such as those described above will result in even more restrictions upon individual rights. The Chinese example can be looked upon in two ways. On the one hand, one could argue that more individual rights have occurred because at least women have some avenues of protest even if in the end they may still have the power of the state imposed upon them (the suspicion is that back in the glory days of the Great Leap Forward even those limited rights did not exist). Yet compared to the rights existent in the Western democracies, it does not seem like much. Yet to be resolved is to what degree organizational change can affect and improve individual rights in the long run.

Recognizing the limitations of participative structures, because of the fact that they too can be used in an autocratic manner, does not negate their usefulness in designing Third World change institutions of the twenty-first century. As with any change process, one must be vigilant for human rights abuses and proceed with the intent that abuses will not occur.

The following section will describe some of the behavioral technologies that can be used within democratic organizations in developing more effective structures in Third World countries.

SPECIFIC BEHAVIORAL TECHNOLOGIES AND HOW THEY CAN BE APPLIED

Given that a change organization is committed to modifying its own mission so that it can more effectively serve the people it is responsible to, there are a number of behavioral technologies that can be utilized to improve the organization's effectiveness.

In the following sections, a number of those technologies will be discussed, and in the notes section at the end of the chapter, additional techniques will be briefly presented. The specific techniques to be described are T-group and administration rehabilitation, group decision making, and interpretive structural modeling and will be presented in consecutive order.

AN INTRODUCTION TO GROUPS, T-GROUPS, AND THE DIFFICULTY OF CHANGE

It is important to realize, in making a major organizational change, that the key actors in the process (the people who function within the organization) can, in fact, be changed from their present behavior to a new behavior that will be more effective in achieving the objectives of the organization. However, there are significantly different schools of thought on how to achieve that.

From the psychoanalytic school, change is largely an internal process where one's behavior is determined by complex internal forces, unconscious defense systems, and underlying causes sometimes created during early childhood by the ill-effects of improper parenting, which dictate the overt behavior or, in some cases, neurosis of the individual. A way of changing individual behavior based on the psychoanalytic model is through the use of the classic therapist-client approach.

There are several things wrong with utilizing that model for organizational change in the Third World. First, using the approach is not only extremely time consuming and expensive, but increasingly we are told it does not really work. While it may make clients more comfortable with themselves, it does not really change them all that much (especially in a short time span such as eight weeks). Secondly, even if it were effective, there are not enough therapists in the world to affect the numbers of people one has to change in order to make a large-scale impact upon organizations in the Third World. Given that the average time to effect change through the therapist is somewhere on the order of five years, the critical deadline for effecting world development by the beginning of the twenty-first century could hardly be attained.

Consequently, the underlying theoretical construct for organizational change, advocated by this book, is to utilize the group social organizational and cultural factors that effect individual behavior and emphasize behavioral modification. The individual occupies a position within a structure (both social and organizational), and behavioral methods utilizing that theoretical philosophy can be brought to bear that can effect change in individuals at both an economy of scale and an efficient cost-benefit ratio. A necessity of any effective model of organizational change is that it be cost efficient. Approaches that, while theoretically sound, require an exorbitant investment may be nice to read about but can never be effectively utilized.

The behavioral modification change process is particularly valuable because one can utilize the *group* as the focus of change both by people within the organization who must be trained and changed and ultimately by groups of clients or beneficiaries to be serviced by the change organization. The investment in group development also nicely fits into the use of linking-pin organizational structures.

Consequently, use of the group for the change process becomes a more logical, cost-effective means for effecting change in the individual. There are several benefits that are aptly described by Marguilies:

the group context for change permits a variety of experiences that the two person, expert-client relationship lacks. First of all, in the context of the group, the person must deal with a variety of other individuals. As a consequence the full range of his coping . . . and defensive strategies for dealing with others is more likely to become evident. Secondly, feedback about his behavior may be gained more easily from a number of participant-observers than from a single person.[4]

An advantage in terms of rapidly effecting change through this multiple feedback process is that it "may be possible to minimize and ignore feedback from one other person; it is quite difficult to dismiss uniform and consistent perceptions from many people."[5] Additionally, the group context for change permits the client to learn by observing the interactive styles of others. Consequently, the group setting provides a mode of very rapid change when it is properly facilitated and monitored.

It has been recognized that the social context that clients reenter (their home organization) must also be changed if efforts upon the individual either through a one-to-one client-professional relationship or through a behavioral modification, group context environment are to be effective.

Consequently, in organizational change intervention strategies, the simple reality is that for change to be effective there must be a total commitment by the highest levels of authority within the organization to support change efforts at the lowest levels. The reason is fairly obvious for, without the formally expressed support of the highest level, lower-level staff members would be foolish to extend themselves in the questioning process that is necessary for effective change for fear that they might be fired by displeased superiors.

AN EXAMPLE OF T-GROUP TRAINING

Change efforts have been tried using group analysis procedures, for example, in some international organizations, but the results have been mixed. Once again, this is primarily due to the lack of top management support but is sometimes related to the lack of a well-designed change strategy. Such efforts tend to be hazardous at best. A specific case in point is an international development organization that I worked with that has engaged in a seven-year group change process to train lower-level operatives in an overall organization change effort.

The training has been in line with what is generally called T-group training. I will diverge from describing the organization's efforts in order to define and examine the nature of T-groups. The T in T-group stands for training and generally can be traced to the work of Kurt Lewin in the late 1940s. Through a variety of experimental efforts in group behavior, he found that the small group is an effective learning device. Many of the reasons for that effectiveness were explained in the previous section describing individual versus small group and social contact change efforts. The key element is that individuals learn much about their own behavior by participating in and using the group as a subject for analysis. The consequence of that individual learning behavior, as a result of interaction within the group process, is to integrate that learning into one's daily organizational life. Lewin called that process "unfreezing" or removing old improper individual attitudes through the group revelation process. One then refreezed new and improved group-determined attitudes within the individual's overt behavior.

A major problem with the use of T-groups is that, while they can be extremely effective as a self-awareness tool, if they are not properly integrated into the design of an organizational change effort, they might not be all that effective in carrying out the organizational change even though they might be extremely enlightening to certain individuals participating in the specific exercises. As mentioned earlier, the organization must clearly have its objectives in mind before it can effectively integrate training into the change strategy. While that may seem a tautological warning, it is, nevertheless, a warning that is often not heeded.

For example, consider an organization that had a goal to increase productivity within the organization's operations. It would be necessary first to establish what kind of and the degree of productivity the organization wishes to achieve. It would be necessary to sit down with the training leaders and translate these specific objectives so that the trainer could then develop a set of exercises that would reinforce those objectives. At this point, the orientation of the writer often runs in direct conflict with the "pure" state of T-group exercises.

In a pure T-group, a trainer or facilitator of the process refuses either to accept or act in a traditional authority role. Group members are left on their own to figure out a way to develop their own authority relationship and then ultimately receive some direction by the trainer once the group has resolved the authority issue on its own terms—that is, if the group is intact, having been left to flounder about on its own.

The problem with the "pure" approach is that refusal of the facilitator to provide any direction to group members in the initial stages can result in group hostility toward the trainer, which can impair or destroy the beneficial intent of the exercise. It has been observed that lack of direction can so greatly impair group effectiveness that the exercise becomes a group effort to denounce the leader. While such a consequence does illustrate the effectiveness of group interaction (a concerted effort to impugn an authority figure), it certainly is not functional for an effective training environment.

Not accepting an authority role for training First World groups of participants can be confusing enough even in an educational environment where participants often have an existing understanding of the deliberate, disorienting efforts of such training. It would be even more difficult to implement in a Third World environment. Imagine the effect of such an approach—a trainer sitting silently, saying nothing (as purist T-group trainers do) with a group of Bolivian agriculture extension agents—all being members of the Quechua-speaking culture who traditionally look to formal leader authority. They would be polite, but they in turn would do nothing and nothing would happen.

Consequently, the use of such training techniques as T-groups must acknowledge the differential effects of culture upon its use. Direct transfer without some modification will probably be ineffective. Therefore, it is advisable that T-group approaches in the international context will require a modified approach, one in which some direction is provided to the group to aid the individual in understanding ambiguity and uncertainty and one in which the effect of culture is considered. More on the effect of cultural differences upon Western developed organizational change approaches will be presented in Chapter 3.

Returning from this rather lengthy discussion of T-groups to the earlier example of the international change agency, it is important to understand the major reason why the training effort failed. The majority of the staff perceived that, because top management was not directly involved in the change process, they were not committed to the change process and were more or less going along with the idea because it seemed fashionable and the consultants were reasonably priced. Consequently, participants hedged a great deal in the exercises, even though the T-group sessions were ultimately modified to permit the trainers to behave as authority figures and team facilitators. It was generally recognized to be a waste of time. In the end, the staff was vindicated, because it became abundantly clear that top management personnel were not concerned about what came out of the training they authorized and, in fact, never participated in any of the training. The seven-year effort was ended with little fanfare.

A word of warning, then, which will be repeated throughout this text, is that if management is not sincere and committed to effecting a real change, then such change efforts are largely a waste of time. Such agencies would do better giving that money to CARE, which would assure, at least, that some of the beneficiaries of the organization would get something out of it.

But once group processes are initiated in the organizational change effort, other group techniques such as group decision making can be developed.

COMPONENTS OF GROUP PROBLEM DIAGNOSIS AND SOLUTION

A classical way of solving organizational problems is first to identify the problem, then to determine possible solutions, and finally to evaluate these alternatives to develop specific solution(s). In this section the classic process and a discussion of how that process can be used by groups will be presented.

The basic elements of group problem diagnosis and solving consist of five steps: problem identification, criteria formulation, alternative solution development, evaluation of possible solutions (matrix evaluation by group consensus), and implementation of a group-developed solution.[6]

Problem Identification

Problem identification would require group members to investigate the total system by interviewing a number of key clients to establish what the clients feel are the primary problems within the organization. After that individual process of interviewing had been carried out, the group members would pool all the information they had gathered and divide on a group basis which of the key problem or problems they would address. Having determined the problem, criteria relevant to the problem would need to be formulated.

Criteria Formulation

Once a problem has been defined and agreed upon through the group decision-making process, the criteria affecting the development of solutions to the problem must be defined. The definition of criteria, in this problem solution process, is that criteria are standards or judgments used to evaluate the suitability of a solution to the problem. It can be also viewed as a constraint that can hinder or prevent the implementation of a solution to a problem.

The primary reason for needing to establish criteria is so that the group will know the boundaries within which they can develop solutions to the problem. For example, if a group did not know the criteria for implementing a solution to a problem, and developed a truly wonderful solution that cost $2 million and took two years to implement, it would be chagrined to find out afterward that the essential criterion was that no solution could cost more than $2,000 and should be implemented within two weeks. Without criteria you cannot construct an effective solution to a problem because you would not know the limitations to your solution development.

Group members establish these criteria boundaries and constraints by interviewing key administrative officials within the organization.

Alternative Solution Development

Solutions to problems are the focus of an organizational design effort. In the case of this book, the concern would be to develop solutions that would focus on the use of management training and improvement in human relations as a vehicle to promote organizational change. Examples of how this would be incorporated into the change effort will be provided in Chapter 6, where actual training exercises are provided. In fact, Chapter 6 will illustrate how one develops an organizational change framework all the way from problem formulation to the development of a management training format to the problem. However, note that the organizational design process is not limited just to training and human relations approaches. The group problem formulation process and criteria development approach can be used for diagnosing and resolving other nonpersonnel problems such as accounting procedures, marketing strategies, and other more routine management problems.

Once solutions have been developed, a quantitative evaluation process (typically a matrix) is used to determine the suitability of a solution.

Matrix Evaluation

After solutions have been developed, the final step of the process is to evaluate the suitability of the solution through some sort of evaluation. A way of going about this is to proceed with a matrix evaluation process where the effect of criteria upon solutions is given weighted values and where the highest total weight value represents the best solution to the problem. Operations research personnel would use the Keppner Trego matrix evaluation process, which utilizes a weighting process of solutions by criteria to determine a highest total weight for the best solution.

An example of the matrix evaluation process is presented below.

Analysis of Problem A

Problem A was analyzed by a group team, and upon further investigation criterias C_1, C_2, and C_3 were determined. Solutions A and B were then developed, analyzed, and weighted by the group to determine their suitability, subject to the constraints of these criteria. The weighting process proceeds as follows. A value of 5 means that the criterion does not constrain the implementation of the solution at all. A value of 0 means that the criterion constrains the solution so much that it would be impossible to implement. The values 1, 2, 3, and 4 indicate greater to lesser degrees of constraint, the values of 1 and 2 being greater, the values of 3 and 4 lesser.

After the weighting analysis has taken place, the weight values are added, and the highest numerical value indicates the best match of a solution. Using the higher values as the best match is an arbitrarily determined procedure. One could have equally made the procedure have the smallest total value be the most appropriate value.

A schematic of the weighting process is presented in Table 2.1.

TABLE 2.1
Example of a Matrix Evaluation: Problem A

Criteria Differential Values	$\cdot 10$	1	1	Simple total weight	Differential total weight
Criteria	C_3	C_2	C_1		
Solution A	1	5	5	11	20
Solution B	3	1	2	6	33

One can see that solution A did not have all that much constraint from the three criteria since the weight values were mostly high. Solution B, on the other hand, had a great deal of constraint since all the weight values were low. According to the procedure, the highest value is 11 and solution A is the most appropriate.

In the weighting process, groups evaluate each solution to the criteria and determine the group weight (this can also be done on an individual basis, but the emphasis of this chapter is to use groups in a participative, organizational setting). There are several procedural ways by which group members can determine these values—all are dependent upon open discussion. First, people can discuss each criterion and use a simple majority vote for each weight. Second, they can rely upon discussion until a consensus or majority agreement is reached on each weight, or they can use a nominal group approach where each solution/criterion weighting would be briefly discussed, and then a rank-ordering of weights would be used to determine the outcome. Because of the secret vote process and reiterations of a vote, nominal group theory can be very time consuming. An effective modification is to use an open discussion, facilitated by a team leader, to determine majority agreement. It is both the fastest and most workable alternative, given that group members agree to follow the basic parliamentary rules of such a procedure. A training exercise illustrating that process is presented in Chapter 6.

Matrix evaluation is a bit more complex than the simple weight determination illustrated earlier. The problem lies in that the criteria for the simple model assume that all criteria are equal in value. That is seldom true, for usually some criteria are considered more important than others and would have a higher value in the evaluation process.

There are two ways to determine the differential values of the criteria. First, on a group or individual basis, a hierarchy of the criteria from most important to least important would be determined such as:

$$\begin{aligned} C_3 &= 10 \\ C_2 &= 1 \quad = \text{Criteria differential weight values} \\ C_1 &= 1 \end{aligned}$$

Criterion C_3 would be the most important and criterion C_1 the least important. Then a value of one would be given to criterion C_1 and the group could be asked to compare the other two criteria and indicate how many times more important each criterion is in comparison to criterion C_1. In this case, it was determined that criterion C_3 is ten times more important than C_1 and criteria C_2 is equal in value to C_1.

A problem with this analysis is that it is subject to bias, especially on an individual basis. Utilizing a group with all its checks and balances would help eliminate individual bias but could introduce a group bias, particularly if the group became subject to "groupthink." A mathematical way of determining hierarchies in a bias-free manner (using groups) is with the use of the interpretive structural modeling technique, which is presented later in this chapter.

Once the differential values of the criteria have been determined, one can then factor those values into the matrix evaluation. Return to the original matrix diagram (Table 2.1), and look at the differential criteria weights. Multiply each differential by the solution/criterion weight, and then add those weights for the differential total weight. Looking at solution A gives a total of 10×1, plus 1×5, plus 1×5 for a differential total of 20. Solution B gives a total of 10×3, plus 1×1, plus 1×2 for a total of 33.

The reason for including the differential weights is clearly indicated in the matrix diagram. By assuming that the criteria are all equal in value, one would recommend solution A because the simple total weight has the highest value of 11. But when you include the differential value of the criteria, one finds a totally different story. Solution B with a total value of 33 is, in fact, the appropriate solution to the problem. The differential value determination is, therefore, an assurance that one does not recommend the wrong solution. It is rare that there is a difference between the simple total weight and the differential total weight, but the difference comes up often enough to require a check to be sure.

A final note is to warn the reader that this kind of analysis, as a technique, is simple and straightforward. However, it is only as good as the information that is brought into it. This is one reason why reliance upon this kind of technique with individual technicians in organizations too often has been worthless since it is very easy to bias the information and the analysis. Using a group of divergent people including technicians, beneficiaries, and managers certainly increases the chances for conflict and a disorderly process, but when facilitated properly it does assure that all relevant information will be acquired and analyzed through the routine checks and balances of the group process. The possibility, then, of producing solutions that match the concerns of all participants is certainly greater than if the process were left to a restricted number of technicians who had no basic responsibility to other participants or beneficiaries.

Solution Implementation

The ultimate step of the process is to implement the solution into the organization. In the case of organizational change, one would need to carry out the individual member training that will make the design of the change effective. Specific training exercises to develop that kind of group member will be detailed in Chapter 6. A key element in carrying out an effective organizational change is to have all those elements necessary to the change process defined and controlled. As stated earlier in the chapter, having the total commitment of top management would also be necessary to insure that the effort would ultimately be implemented within the change organization, instead of being an exercise in futility parallel to the international organization illustrated in an earlier section.

As a more specific example of the process, the flow of developing a solution to resolve a problem, is presented in the following section.

A Specific Problem Analysis

Problem Definition

The problem-solving group determined that extension agents are insensitive to the cultural practices of the people they serve. These people, consequently, no longer will listen to what the agents have to say.

Criteria Formulation

The problem-solving group, in consultation with top management, has been told that it must match the following criteria in any solution it develops.

C_1 = The cost cannot go beyond \$50,000.

C_2 = Improvement must occur within six months.

C_3 = Extension agents must become culturally sensitive and once again able to work with people in the field.

Alternate Solution Development

The first solution was to hire expatriate trainers to retrain the agents. Upon investigation, the group found that it would cost \$150,000, would take two years, and would involve the use of "purist" T-group trainers from Berkeley, California, who refused to behave as authority figures and who insisted that all participants must sit in hot tubs, quietly chanting their personal mantra throughout the training.

The second solution was to bring in some of the people who had complained about the behavior of the extension agents, get their input about the incident and their knowledge of the cultural behavior in the region, and make them members of the team. With the help of the resident organization design specialist, the decision-making group, and field representatives, a training program would be developed at no cost except for a nominal payment to the field people who participated in the design sessions.

Matrix Evaluation

Top management evaluated the solutions by comparing each solution with the three criteria. The second solution was found to best match those criteria and was thus chosen as the solution to adopt.

Solution Implementation

The second solution used the innovative approach of allowing field beneficiaries to be trainers especially in training personnel to understand the culture of the people they served. The experiment was hailed as a success and was emulated by other change agencies in the country.

In essence, this is in the process. While it is relatively simple, analytically it is only as effective as the quality and concern of the effort that goes into it. There are many criticisms of the process, which will be explored in the following section.

Criticism of the Classical Design of the Change Process

The previous description of how to analyze a problem, and come to some sort of decision based upon that logical spread of the assorted elements, is not particularly unique. It is, in fact, commonly used as a bureaucratic procedure for routine planning within an organization. But as a tool for making decisions that will be effective, for example, serving beneficiaries in a rural development program, it may have serious drawbacks. The reason is that, when it is done by bureaucrats within an organization, it can too often lack the reality test that is provided by incorporating the input of the people that planned programs will eventually benefit. Korten describes a number of weaknesses that can be produced by relying solely upon the internal, rational model:

1. "The tools of the planners are not sufficiently powerful to handle the range of data. . . . As a result the analysis of the planners is at best partial . . . the needs and desires of the common people are particularly prone to neglect."

2. "Important decisions are seldom if ever made by unitary decision-makers on the basis of purely technical analysis." Effective decisions require the involvement and working through of all the parties affected (beneficiaries) if they are to be workable in the end.

3. "Organizations, which have to implement those decisions, may be demoralized by decisions inappropriate to the local conditions of the people they serve."[7]

All of these criticisms of the rational process are valid, and perhaps even to the degree that Korten feels, namely, that such an approach forces "decision-making processes into a mold that is inherently unworkable in addressing all but the most routine of governmental activities."[8] However, I would not be quite as critical since much of my experience has been with organizations that do not even use that degree of rigor, limited as it is, in their decision-making process. In other words, planning and organizational change are more often an ad-hoc affair. As an example, in a study for the Organization of American States (OAS), it was found that virtually none of the planning agencies in over 11 countries had any real planning or organizational change capability among the staff. In fairness, that does not mean there had been no effort to build that capability. The OAS, in fact, provides training workshops for staff in member countries. The problem focuses more on the marketability of people who receive such training (by private industry) and their movement from public to private organizations.

These criticisms, however, do not mean that such techniques are not useful, and probably Korten would agree. They merely illustrate that some modification must be made so that the final product can be used effectively. A primary way of doing that is by taking the process away from the individual or the internal professional group and using it with a representative group as was presented in the earlier description of group problem diagnosis and solution.

Instead of relying solely upon professionals within the organization, the decision-making body should include at least one representative from the outside group of beneficiaries to lend a field-based reality to the decision-making process. These people should not be token members tolerated as a symbolic gesture that participation is valued and promoted by the organization, but rather must be trained in the same skills as the organization's professional members. Just because the field representative(s) may be relatively uneducated does not mean that they cannot be trained to understand and interact with relatively sophisticated decision-making tools. To illustrate that point, a section later in the chapter will show how illiterate farmers are capable of using a rather sophisticated decision-making tool in group decision making.

Even U.S. business corporations are beginning to realize the advantages of incorporating beneficiaries in the decision-making and problem-solving process. For example, as indicated in the *Harvard Business Review,* "by giving employees at all levels an opportunity to participate in shaping a meaningful group problem diagnosis and then feeding back the results to them, management can open both upward and downward communication channels."[9] The article then describes how the results are used by employers to develop realistic solutions to the problems identified by the survey results. While the thrust of the approach is still to dominate the control of decision-making by management, it is, nevertheless, a thrust in the direction of greater participation, analogous to what has been proposed in this section.

The primary point is that the use of participative approaches in the developmental process allows all the members affected by the change effort to contribute to the change process and increases the likelihood that an effective program will be created, which furthermore will be supported by the people it serves.

EXAMPLE OF A RELATIVELY SOPHISTICATED GROUP DECISION-MAKING TECHNIQUE—INTERPRETIVE STRUCTURAL MODELING

The author carried out an experiment in group decision making with a number of illiterate Mexican farmers, to find out whether relatively uneducated participants could effectively interact with a fairly sophisticated group analysis and decision-making technique.

The particular decision-making technique involved is called interpretive structural modeling (ISM). Basically what one can do with the technique is to form hierarchies of elements, or variables, and using a group decision-making process (through a binary analysis matrix procedure), establish the importance or lack of importance of certain elements. Defining this a bit more technically,"ISM involves taking a set of variables (elements), comparing these variables in a defined, orderly relation, constructing a binary matrix from the comparisons, and deriving graphs which in a simple, visual schematic shows whatever hierarchical properties the original act of elements possesses."[10] In simple terms, the procedure is a quantitative means of determining what are the most important things (positive or negative) that can affect an organizational change effort. It can be used as a client-based information source.

The setting of the experiment was the introduction of biogas generators in Mexico that met a fair deal of resistance in the original introduction of the system to farmers. It was hypothesized that several variables might be affecting the potential receptivity of the system. Variables included cost, complexity, preference to use wood instead of methane gas produced by the system, and so on.[11]

Farmers were organized into small groups, and on a group basis went through the matrix evaluation process, producing a hierarchy of variables deemed, by the group, as most important to the adoption of the technology. As reported in the original publication on the study,

Use of the method presented few problems and the farmers who had no knowledge of set theory or in many cases even simple arithmetic, interacted extremely well with the matrix evaluation procedures. What was of particular interest was the participants' abilities to keep the numerous combinations in mind without creating errors. Typically, educated people start using their own systems which come in conflict with the logic of the process. Once the farmers understood the rules, they seldom committed errors.[12]

That was some years ago, and while ISM is an interesting evaluation technique, it is basically irrelevant since the real success behind the experiment was that farmers were organized in group decision-making units and also knew that their comments and beliefs (as expressed during the exercise) would be included in the final recommendations to managers in the regional agricultural program. Had this experiment been done on an individual basis, with no understanding that the participant was being given a decision-making capacity in a regional project, one could expect that there would have been less facility in getting through the exercise. Participation, group process, and responsibility were the key factors, not the ISM technique.

The importance of the experiment was to show that group decision-making processes can lead to the development of effective solutions to organizational change efforts. Specific quantitative techniques such as ISM are irrelevant other than to illustrate that uneducated people can deal quite easily with relatively sophisticated (albeit irrelevant) quantitative techniques. The power lies in properly managed group decision making and participation. This is a point that will be reinforced throughout the remainder of the book.

FINAL COMMENTS ON BEHAVIORAL TECHNOLOGIES

There are many additional planning techniques that can be utilized in the change process. They cannot all be described in this book, so the emphasis will be on presenting behavioral technologies. In the notes section of this chapter, a number of bureaucratic planning techniques and references for detailed explanations of them are provided.[13]

Two issues that intimately affect the use of behavioral or bureaucratic techniques must be emphasized. If administrators do not understand the technology, they cannot use it effectively. Consequently, there is a vital need to control this variable either through hiring practices or retraining. The second point is that, in creating effective organizational designs for the twenty-first century, the group process is the primary means to develop new institutions that can effectively serve beneficiaries. The shoddy record of the past three decades has illustrated clearly that centralized plans or programs, developed in a vacuum, do not work. To be effective, we must include the input of the people served, even though that can be inconvenient at times.

If we are to be concerned with developing twenty-first century designs, we must also be concerned with some of the parameters that effect that development. Such parameters include the effect of inadequately trained administrators, the kind of training necessary to rehabilitate existing organizations, the kind of strategies needed to be effective in initiating change, and some of the cultural biases that may occur in the training efforts to effect those changes.

THE EFFECT OF INADEQUATELY TRAINED ADMINISTRATORS

In the introduction to this book, it was stated that, to some extent, the organizational changes that we are capable of initiating now could not have been done on a large scale in the 1950s and 1960s. The reason is that the number of administrators capable of understanding the complex underlying behavior in implementing change did not exist, at least in sufficient numbers to be effective.

The lack of adequately trained administrators is still a major problem, but unlike the 1950s and 1960s there exists a much larger corps of people who do understand the behavioral side of the change process. If they are not already in a position of power to effect change, they will certainly be in a position where they can support their comrades who have reached that position. It goes without saying that unless administrators have an understanding of how to implement the change process effectively, and of the group or team effort involved, as well as the need for participation by beneficiaries, there is a rather high likelihood that the results will be disappointing. "Training of the people who participate in these key team decision-making units is again of central importance."[14] Korten's assessment of the nature of this training is appropriate:

1. "Administrative behavior needs to be redefined. This may require a redefinition of administrative roles form administrator to facilitator-trainer." This, of course, requires a training function in itself. To be able to change that administrative behavior will require altering the existing behavior of administrators or hiring new administrators who exhibit the appropriate behavior. (As described earlier in this chapter, the rehabilitation of autocratic administrators can be a difficult or impossible task).

2. "Train professional analysts [who would be part of the group decision-making team] to give attention to organizational issues, and social outcomes . . . in their evolution of policy options." In this context, the members of the target beneficiary group would also become professional analysts, would be given the same training, and would become members of the team.

3. "Train decision-makers in the use of economic, social, and organizational analysis, to increase their ability to use the contributions of specialized analysts."[15]

Certainly, these sorts of adaptations will be useful to the group decision-making process, but they alone will not assure success. To be effective in the field, the beneficiaries of the organization have to be involved intimately. Without a sincere commitment to that objective by the organization during its change efforts, it is likely that one will see, again, an inappropriate development of solutions to beneficiary problems—a continuation of developmental practices as they were conducted in earlier decades. With the advent of the twenty-first century upon us, we cannot afford (if we ever could) the practice of organizational change in a vacuum.

The intent, then, of this chapter has not been to reject the more classical approaches to decision making. The basic techniques, after all, are still relevant to group decision making and are relevant to the process of changing organizations. However, in talking about organizational change to fit a twenty-first century world, one must recognize the necessity for beneficiary input and for problem solving that involves all members of the spectrum (rather than continuing to use the archaic approach whereby experts find solutions on behalf of members in the system). For a truly developed world and effective solutions, organizational bureaucrats will have to accept that they are no more important and do not understand the particular situation any better than the target group they work for. If they do not already use that approach, they will have to be adequately trained so they will function properly, within a new developmental order.

When one analyzes the above statements, knowing the personality characteristics of most bureaucrats, one has some idea of the amount of training required to change today's typical organizational bureaucrat. Some people feel they can only be changed by mechanisms of "extreme prejudice."

Yet no less a commitment must be made if, in fact, Third World development is to become a reality. The people who will manage the process, both institutional administrators as well as beneficiary participants, will make or break that effort. Both will have to work together and will have to understand the basic elements of participative change approaches.

WOMEN AS THE ORGANIZATIONAL CHANGE AGENTS OF THE TWENTY-FIRST CENTURY

One view of why we have so many organizational problems in the world is because of the prominent role of men. Their unrelenting quest for power and dominance results in autocratic, organizational structures, and their use of power and authority is a means of controlling and directing people. There is a natural propensity for men to form hierarchical institutions and dominate not only lesser members of their own sex but, even more so, women. Through history, women have been viewed as inferior by men although they have consistently been the mainstays of subsistence and of maintaining the family throughout the world.

The natural ability of women to cooperate and to work effectively in small groups strongly suggests that there should be greater emphasis on involving them in the process of organizational change. Not only are they better at using behavioral technology, but there is also a greater likelihood that they will really become involved in achieving the objectives of the change organization in the field setting since it is they who hold the family together in all cultures of the world.

At the present time, however, "men own 99% of the world's property and earn 90% of its wages, while producing only 55% of the world's food and performing only one third of the world's work. Men rather exclusively direct the course not just of states and corporations but of culture: religion, arts, education."[16] The dominance of men in running all kinds of institutions further stacks the deck in favor of man's autocratic behavior to the detriment of carrying out effective change in the Third World. "Most men in Western societies work in some form of institution. Institutions breed competitiveness and inculcate an instrumental relation to everything, even personal relationships. One has contacts, not friends. One chooses to cultivate people not (as many women do) because of a sense of rapport with them, but because they might be useful."[17] But this is all learned behavior, and men can be taught differently, should a culture change its view of male-female relationships.

Research is showing, at least in the United States, that women may be superior as managers because of their very ability to work together better, to have a greater degree of sympathy, sensitivity, and concern for human relations, and to create a good working climate. These attributes make them superior managers particularly in service economies that rely upon flexibility and creativity rather than on rigid, drill sergeant managers. Even motherhood affects women's ability as managers since raising children teaches the arts of compromise, conciliation, listening, and crisis management. Motherhood also provides on-the-job training in operant conditioning, through the use of positive reinforcement in raising children. These life skills are invaluable to managers—and some would also say applicable to dealing with the childlike behavior of male counterparts. While Ashley Montagu's classic book, *Natural Superiority of Women*, has been in circulation for over 30 years, it is only recently that men have begun to recognize that there is actually something to it.

Chapter 1 stated that all efforts to change organizations were basically meaningless in the face of a lack of power or commitment at higher policy levels to support significant change efforts. The feminist literature would say that this lack of commitment emerges because men are in charge and will not make a commitment to a more participative, sensitive, humanistic approach to organizational change.

The change to participative, positive-reinforced change approaches can be viewed as feminine because feminists specifically call for removal of the old dominance power plays common to male/organizational environments. A feminine orientation substitutes a more nurturing, flexible environment that is more conducive to long-term success and commitment by all the participants. From the viewpoint of most males, this is revolutionary thinking, far more threatening then a communist takeover—a communist takeover would be male after all.

The reality of male dominance undoubtedly has had an effect on the development of management systems for a long period of time. For example, in the culture of the industrial revolution, we had men giving orders, not only to other men, but to women. The pattern was a rigid patriarchical, "do as I say now or get out" process. French reports that, during the early years of the industrial revolution, women who objected were routinely raped in the industries where they worked.

This pattern persists in some contemporary cultures. In India it is the male who dictates the management style. Women largely stay locked up at home, still locked in age-old patterns of purdah. In Latin America the order of machismo means an autocratic, military style of behavior in which subordinates do what they are told—feedback and communication are irrelevant. Both cultures are specifically antiwomen in their outlook. Despite specific legislative action, the United States is really not all that different.

On a worldwide basis, it is probably not difficult to understand the underlying reason why male-dominated organizations resist a more feminist (if you will) move to more communication, participation, and concern about the people to be helped—it is not a manly view of how to do things. John Wayne, after all, would not stop for feedback or give much praise in the resolution of a problem. He would just charge ahead, probably to the disadvantage of some group—usually women or American Indians.

There will be a need to overcome a totally male-dominated developmental approach and to recognize the highly effective role that women can play in organizational change. It will be interesting to test out that theory in the Philippines with Cory Aquino, who by most observers is considered thoroughly feminine in her outlook and who talks a great deal about introducing participation in the reconstruction of the country. However,.other examples of woman-directed leadership, Thatcher in England and Gandhi in India, have not followed that pattern. Their ineffectiveness has much to do with male dominance of their political systems. Aquino has the chance and the power to change all that, as she consolidates the support of her people and makes organizational changes.

In summation, it is a fact that women are far superior to men in participative management, group development, and overall sensitivity to the necessary conflict that must occur in a complex change process. Subsequent chapters will further reinforce the view that women may well be the prime (and appropriate) innovators in developing and implementing organizational designs for the twenty-first century.

A CAUTIONARY NOTE

Over the years there has been much concern that the use of behavioral technology has an associated ethical issue to it—that improper use may result in the conditioning of people and the furtherance of totalitarian societies. The potential for that kind of abuse does exist, and the earlier section on China tends to support that belief since the use of small-group pressure does result in changing a woman's behavior (in that case) to accept an abortion she does not want. But so does autocratic behavior as practiced in Western societies. If an academic administrator says a nontenured professor has to teach four classes at eight in the morning, and smile while doing so, that professor will probably do so, especially if he or she has no alternative. As an abuse of power, there is little difference in the short run. But in the long run, the small group presents a greater opportunity for freedom and democracy than autocratic control ever will.

The ethical concern, obviously, is that as we create the organizational designs of the twenty-first century we must eliminate the abuses. The technology in itself does not create the problem; it is the use of the technology by the wrong people in the wrong environment that creates the problem. Nobody is suggesting that this is going to be easy to accomplish.

SUMMARY

The argument has been made in this chapter that the management of the change process can benefit by the use of behavioral technology. Furthermore, behavioral technology that utilizes the small group as a decision-making unit can be more effective especially when such a group is composed of representatives of both the change organization and the people it serves. This is basically a restatement of what Elton Mayo and Learned Rothlisberger concluded in their classic "Hawthorne Studies" in the 1920s. The Hawthorne Studies are considered to be the birth of participative management, and the basic tenet is that people support what they have helped to create. It seems an almost obvious tautology, yet for the majority of change organizations it is still far from self-evident.

The relevance of 60-year-old findings indicates a positive reality for changing organizations and creating designs for the twenty-first century. Since the technology already exists, all we need to do is apply what we already know about human behavior in organizational settings. There is no need for a crash effort in research for the knowledge has been around for some time. In fact, if one wanted to get really technical about the origins of behavioral technology such as participative management and operant conditioning, one could study the writings of Jesus and the conduct of his disciples. It was very open, very trusting, very participative, and just as described in the earlier example of the manipulative informer in today's quality circles, it was betrayed by an informer, Judas, who abused the democracy and freedom of his circle for the autocratic power of the Roman state. Without getting too religious for the reader, organizational change, quality circles, and behavioral technology have been around for a long time—possibly from the dawn of humanity. Human behavior may have been only recently perverted (the last 10,000 years) when man switched from a hunter-gatherer to a "civilized" culture. Certainly we know that the few existing hunter-gatherer societies are very participative, use operant conditioning in their acculturation, and have a more egalitarian view of women's rights and place within the universe.

Women's behavior may be the long-term solution to effecting world development and implementing organizational change. Men certainly have had their chance and are primarily responsible for the present state of world affairs. Women, because of their innate qualities of greater cooperation, nurturing, and overall resilience, are probably in a better position to implement the designs for the twenty-first century. There is a good chance that, with their increasing access to power through the vote and through education, women will play a major role in that change process. Men should welcome a management move in that direction.

A number of behavioral technologies have been described. One could go on for several chapters describing more for the list is extensive. The few that were selected focus on group development, group problem solving, and participation of all the actors in the process of organizational change. This emphasis on multicultural groups is in direct contrast to the professional approach where organizational professionals, without the influence and knowledge base of beneficiaries, would devise the organizational change process. Such an emphasis is, of course, intended since the objective of this book is to convince the reader that, if designs for the twenty-first century are to be effective, they will have to include the involvement of all participants in the process. The nineteenth century reliance on autocracy and top-downward-decision making is over. For the twenty-first century, we must persevere through the sweat, conflict, and discomfort of a bottom-upward, participative development process. As an organizational change specialist, I welcome that reality. The trick is to convince, retrain, and rehabilitate those who presently manage the change organization and who control the power in Third World countries to welcome that reality.

NOTES

1. Warren Bennis, *Changing Organizations* (New York: McGraw-Hill, 1966).
2. Interview with Tonia Papki, Management Development International, New York,

January 1986.

3. Rensis Likert, *The Human Organization* (New York: McGraw-Hill, 1967).

4. Newton Marguilies and John Wallace, *Organizational Change: Techniques and Application* (Glenview, Ill.: Scott, Foresman, 1973).

5. Ibid.

6. A problem with this chapter is that one has to assume that there are ways to develop groups effectively, since groups are the key element in all the behavioral technologies described in the chapter. For those readers who want a preview of the group development process, it is suggested that they skip ahead to Chapter 6 and read the sections on group development training.

For readers who are not already aware of the variety of techniques for internal control, an excellent description is provided in Bryant and White, *Managing Development in the Third World* (Boulder, Colo.: Westview Press, 1982). The following techniques are described: decision-tree diagramming, oval diagramming, project design, feasibility studies, cost-benefit analysis, coordination and control, budgeting, critical-path method, and PERT charting.

The point I am making is that those areas are indeed necessary for the "little people," that is, the petty technicians who value that kind of work for its own sake and do not necessarily care about what it all signifies. As most management professors say, God knows we need accountants (the kind of people who do this kind of work), but keep them chained up so they cannot affect the really serious tasks of an organization.

7. David Korten, "Towards a Technology for Managing Social Development," in *Population and Social Development Management* (Caracas: Instituto de Estudios Superiores de Administracion, 1979), p. 31.

8. Ibid.

9. "Changing Employee Values," *Harvard Business Review* 57 (January-February 1979), p. 124.

10. Allen Jedlicka, "Interpretive Structural Modeling," *Desarrollo Rural en las Americas* 11 (January-April, 1979), p. 20.

11. Ibid.

12. Ibid.

13. An additional list of techniques appropriate to the management of the change process is provided in note 6, along with a specific reference that offers detailed description of those techniques. Bureaucratic planning and design techniques that are necessary to effective *internal* organization maintenance are included.

Consequently, the focus of the book is on the joint mechanisms by which we can merge the focus of innovative managers within the organizations with the forces of the people they serve as a vehicle to design the organization. After the important work is done, one can always unleash the "little people" to crank out the budgeting and scheduling work, carefully locking them up again once the job is done before they try to influence the new design of the organization.

14. Korten, "Toward a Technology," p. 35.

15. Ibid.

16. Marilyn French, *Beyond Power* (New York: Summit Books, 1985).

17. Ibid.

3

Cultural Bias in the Organizational Change Process

A Peruvian, entering heaven stopped to complain to St. Peter about why God gave so many resources to Bolivia—gold, silver, oil—and so little to Peru. Peter rubbed his chin and said, "Ah, but look at the kind of people he put in Bolivia."

Rural villager's comment
on the character
of the urban Bolivian

INTRODUCTION

The old story about Bolivia is appropriate to illustrate the limitations of culture, society, and history in effecting rapid organizational change—for the nature of a country's people still plays a significant role in its lack of progress and change.

Prior to the 1952 revolution, Bolivia still lived in the Middle Ages with a feudal system that traced its origins to the hacienda system of early sixteenth century Spanish colonialism. The majority of the population (still about 80 percent Indian) was owned by the landowner class of more or less pure European blood peoples. On paper, the 1952 revolution changed all that, parceling out the old landholdings to the former "serfs." But culture and history perverted that technical change. The Indians, even though landholders, were still controlled by the former landholders who dominated the economy and the national system. Little was done to make the organizational changes in governmental agencies that could help Indians become an integrated part of society—they were still *indios gran puta,* dumb Indian whores.

I do not want to give the impression that the cultural and historical effects on change occur negatively only in countries like Bolivia. One has only to look at the dismal last 100 years of the United States, with it failure to integrate blacks after the Civil War, to recognize that culture and history affect all countries. Given that Bolivia actually is now, 30 years after the revolution, making serious efforts to integrate the Indian shows that their response has been somewhat faster than that of the United States, but there is still a long way to go before attitudes toward the majority Indian population completely change.

The point to be made is that, in organizational change efforts, past culture and history can affect the success of the change efforts in the form of individual behavior or specific individuals who will behave inappropriately with the beneficiaries they serve. The point was made in Chapter 2 that there are ways (such as T-group training) to change those preexisting attitudes into more useful ones. But for some people it will not work, and the solution will probably have to be replacement by appropriate personnel. One of the most successful countries in resolving this variable has been China through its revolutionary process, which, in accordance with Bennis, seems inevitably headed for democracy. The price for that progress, in terms of human life has been high, and cannot be advocated. However, similar processes will continue in countries throughout the world regardless of who advocates or deplores them. Unfortunately, too often "the price of freedom is blood,"[1] and that price will probably continue to be paid right into the next century.

Most of us would not promote an internal revolution such as the one in China. The obvious alternative is peaceful organizational change. There is much that can be done if peace is given a chance provided that we can overcome the limitations of culture and history without a revolution. An additional concern to this process becomes the effect of Western bias as countries collaborate with international sources in the process of effecting organizational change.

WESTERN BIAS IN COLLABORATION WITH HOST COUNTRIES

Twenty years ago, when I first started to work in the area of international development, it was fashionable to say that the end of the millennium would be the day of reckoning, Armageddon, when millions of people would be starving to death and, in line with C. P. Snow's comments, we would watch it all on color television.

Well, things speeded up a bit. We achieved that state considerably earlier with the current events in the Sahel, Ethiopia, the Philippines, and the United States itself, where it is estimated that over 3 million people wander homelessly, with another 40 million subsisting at the poverty line. What is probably not surprising is that it does not really seem all that bad. We seem to accept such a reality without a great deal of distress—even with the assorted live-aid, farm-aid, and band-aid programs that are currently popular.

That very human ability to adjust and accept such a situation may assure that the final chapter of our current state of international relations and responsibility may continue to produce an international behavior that will only make the problem worse in the first half of the twenty-first century—because of the human ability to use selective perception.

One wants to believe that members of the Reagan administration (as an example) are sincere in their desire to help Third World countries. One of those concerns has resulted in the Carribean Basin Initiative, an effort to industrialize the Carribean countries. The initiative has had some success. For example, Haiti is viewed by some authorities as a little Asia in the Carribean, for a number of companies have begun traditional sweatshop industries (footwear, clothing, and crafts) employing directly or indirectly some 300,000 people. Labor is cheap,[2] and products enter the United States duty free through the initiative. A similar story has long existed in the twin factories system along the Mexican border, where even the U.S. managers of those companies admit that they are exploiting Mexican labor at $4 a day as a last ditch effort to compete with Asian labor.[3]

However, in terms of long-term development and the organizational changes that must accompany that process, citizens of those countries are being prepared only for a short-term, industrial revolution experience (not development) that will be replaced as quickly as possible by twenty-first century technological processes (robotics without the human factor) back in the home countries of those expatriate companies. The Third World, after its brief taste of sweatshop industry, will remain undeveloped.

In the short run (it will probably last little longer than about 20 years) nineteenth century organizational structures and reliance upon nineteenth century classical management will provide some low-paying jobs, but there will be no permanence to it, for in the end such companies will move on. These companies provide very little democracy, with people doing the work as defined for them or quickly leaving by request if they object. What is needed is the development of new organization and change approaches that do not reflect the cultural bias of nineteenth century industrial organization. That most likely will not come from international companies.

A major obstacle for developing effective change within the Third World must be surmounted. The problem is that the Western bias of international sources working with Third World counterparts more often promotes inappropriate organizational changes to a nineteenth century behavior (which, of necessity, is being eliminated either through termination of old industrial processes) or by introduction of new organizational approaches).

Many would hail the development of these production-sharing sweatshops as a positive development for Third World countries. However, the continued spread of this phenomenon, since it will prevent the introduction of the organizational changes that are necessary for twenty-first century industry, will once again assure that the Third World remains behind the First World as the transition is made from the twentieth to the twenty-first century.

Certainly one sees this scenario unfolding in Third World industrial development as Third World countries, a source of cheap labor, replace First World industrial jobs. After all, when a U.S. businessman comes to a country like Haiti, possibly escaping a union in his own country, his cultural bias of wanting and in this case getting malleable, nonunion labor that will not question management behavior is probably a natural desire and one that is readily satisfied in a desperate country.

AUTOCRATIC BEHAVIOR IN THIRD WORLD ORGANIZATIONS

When one looks at the behavior of host-country public organizations that deal in rural development, agricultural development, and social development, those autocratic Western biases come into play again. It is often expressed in behavior where the expert consultant tells the host national what is the correct thing to do without, generally, a great deal of input from the consultant's counterpart or the beneficiaries the organization serves. The influence of Western consultants too often primarily benefits only the consultants. It is, after all, convenient to be autocratic. Building democratic organizational forms and promoting participation are time-consuming tasks and full of conflict.

In the case of agriculture, autocratic behavior is largely a reflection of what is done in the United States. The behavior of a U.S. agricultural extension person is mostly top downward with little involvement of the client. Typically, such an agent has a body of knowledge about the kinds of infrastructure inputs one needs and tells the beneficiary farmers how to apply them with little involvement of the recipient in the process. In fact, the United States is only beginning to recognize the shortsightedness of such a development approach in all its economic activities. Recently, as an example, the extension services in the state of California have begun a series of workshops to retrain their extension staff into promoting greater involvement of the farmers they serve in the long-range planning of new agricultural directions the state may take in the twenty-first century. A current view is that, as a consequence of top-downward, capital-intensive agriculture, California may be putting itself into a position where costs (both in inputs and environmental degradation) may make them noncompetitive early in the twenty-first century. Trainers in this program comment that extension agents are extremely resistant to the involvement of beneficiaries in the planning and design process and that many of them will have to be removed one way or the other. Does that sound rather like the Third World? Certainly the Third World has no monopoly on pigheaded behavior, and the United States is no exception. Fortunately, for the United States during the past 30 years, it was possible to dominate the world economy because of its advantageous economic position after World War II. As the other developed countries rebuilt, and the world once again established a global market system (maximizing it somewhere in the late 1970s), our autocratic management systems did not have the flexibility to compete with the more democratic systems of Japan and Europe.

Such autocratic behavior without the input of environmental field information can be partially blamed for the current agricultural problems we face. As an example, extension has promoted high-input agriculture for the past 30 years (the culture of high-input consumption of synthetic fertilizer, herbicides, and pesticides). Now one finds severe nitrate poisoning of water supplies, increasing rates of rare cancer among farmers (suspected to come from the more exotic pesticides), and an agricultural technique that has become too costly for the price that grain pays.

A counterculture of quasi-organic farm techniques, and mixed agriculture using limited amounts of synthetic inputs, is finally beginning to become available to farmers from nonextension organizations, such as those that support organic gardening. Even the U.S. Department of Agriculture (USDA) is starting to pay attention to such trends. But the significant point is that the autocratic, one-sided thrust of extension services has contributed significantly to the problem. With a client-focused program, there is a likelihood that new directions could have been formulated before passing the eleventh hour. Extension agents, had they been client focused, would have been disturbed about reports of funny tasting water and farmer cancer rates and would have addressed the problems sooner. As stated earlier, the state of California recognizes such problems and is introducing client-centered extension. States such as Iowa remain locked in a traditional autocratic mode and probably will not survive.

The final point to be made is that Western bias lends itself to an autocratic "do as I say" approach and needs to be questioned for its suitability not only in Third World countries, but in the country of origin. Not surprisingly, autocratic behavior is also a common problem in Third World countries and too often is reinforced by Western consultants. As outlined in Chapter 2, there are specific tools for preventing the bias to dominate, as seen by the collaborative efforts between Western authorities, host-country authorities, and beneficiaries in the communities the organizations serve.

COMMUNITY PARTICIPATION—CULTURAL ADJUNCTS TO RAPID CHANGE

Francis Korten, in a retrospective view, shows that most developmental agencies came into being in times when participation was not a major theme or a valued "cultural" behavior of an organization.[4] In those earlier days, a centralized service delivery system was built with the idea that it had something valuable to offer to people in the field and that all that was necessary was for professional experts to administer what they had to a passive audience. Since the information was appropriate, there was no need for beneficiary involvement.

Unfortunately, in terms of effecting appropriate change, these past cultural and societal realities still affect the ability to change rapidly to a more participative method of interacting with beneficiaries. Participation requires more than merely saying that organization representatives will behave participatively. As an example of how past cultural practices and Western influence affect organizational changes, the Ujamaa system in Tanzania, initiated under President Julius Nyerere, has been touted as an outstanding example of participative approaches. In the first days of his administration, Nyerere proclaimed:

"When all the power remains at the center, local problems can remain and fester, while local people who are aware of them are prevented from using their initiative in finding solutions. Similarly, it is sometimes difficult for local people to respond with enthusiasm to a call for development work which may be to their benefit, but which has been decided upon and planned by an authority hundreds of miles away."[5]

Subsequently, an impressive, now-historical series of reforms were initiated to increase popular participation from the grassroots level as well as provide more integration of development programs at the local level with, above all, a focus on the decentralization of the national socioeconomic, political, and administrative institutions. It all sounded very nice on paper, but, unfortunately, the program was not executed properly.

Even with all this restructuring of the nation's economic system along the lines of greater participation at the lower levels and the creation of such an economic entity as the Ujamaa village, investigators found several shortcomings. The "reformed" extension people participating in these new structures used a technical language and a still expatriate interaction behavior in dealing with villagers that at best was "overly complicated to an educated, but non-technically oriented mind and which was surely no more than barely comprehensible to semi-literate people."[6]

Who does one blame for such behavior? Certainly, especially in the former European colonies, there has been a Western bias coming from the collaboration of colonial officials and, to a still large extent (especially in the East African countries), from the influence of expatriate professionals working within the country's change organizations. This is, after all, a behavior one associates more often with an educated European dealing with the white man's burden. Educated black men can also behave in a similar manner. The answer, probably, is that the influence of the former colonial masters in this situation is still high. After all, liberation for most African countries is barely 20 years old. The people who were trained in the colonial system are now barely approaching middle age and can be expected to be lodged within the centers of power within their respective countries.

A possible answer, then, to eliminate Western bias is to come up with participatory approaches that are unique expressions of the country's culture. One, however, cannot become self-assured that that is necessarily the best approach to change. One should not belittle all Western approaches just because it has become xenophobically chic to say that anything Western in origin is evil or irrelevant to a developing country. What is needed is to use what is best from the

West and reject what is bad. Two examples of incorporating existing cultural practices with Western practices illustrate this point on a macro level: postwar industrialization in Japan and development of the Ujamaa system in Tanzania.

The Japanese System

Japanese industrial products during the 1950s were considered worse than present-day U.S. products. They were flimsy, nondescript, made with poor-quality materials, and, even worse, tacky. The epithet "Made in Japan" was somewhat of a joke. But, to make a somewhat lengthy story short, beginning in the early 1960s organizational changes incorporating Western practices within the industrial setting played a major role in improving the quality of Japanese products. One of those changes was the introduction of quality circles (briefly described in Chapter 2), which could be defined as a means of allowing participation of the lowest levels in planning and decision making. Circles are particularly effective in Japan because they utilize the cultural reality that the Japanese like to work in groups and by nature use group decision-making processes.

A point to be made is that contrary to many perceptions the origin of quality circles was not Japan, but rather the United States. There was a very strong Western flavor in the development of this organization change device. Basically, quality circles are nothing other than the applied use of the findings of the Western Electric Hawthorne Studies of the late 1920s researched by Learned Rothlisberger and Elton Mayo. In that study, in an effort to show that increased lighting could increase productivity of workers, it was necessary to organize the workers in the experiment into small groups and to allow the experimental groups to interact with the investigators. Ultimately, it was found that the real reason for increased productivity was an organizational change that allowed the worker to contribute to the analysis and planning of the experiment (workers traditionally had worked by themselves and were administered by line authority without the right to contribute to planning or decision making).

Quality circles in the Japanese context are really nothing more than that. Workers are allowed to organize in work teams, and with the help of one member who has been especially trained in facilitating group decisions, daily group meetings are held where workers can share their thoughts on how certain industrial practices can be improved or modified. These suggestions are discussed within the group (which is facilitated by the trained member) and ultimately relayed to higher levels of authority. Various incentives for successful changes are then awarded to the group, such as monetary rewards, company recognition, and vacation days. These rewards are consistent with positive reinforcement and operant conditioning, a behavioral technology that will be discussed in Chapter 4.

There is, of course, a cultural reality that complements the use of small-group quality circles. Japanese culture emphasizes the use of group decision making at all levels of society. A Japanese company, for example, does not have a simple corporate leader at the top who makes the major company decisions. It has a committee of several executives who, with a great deal of effort, laboriously work out a collective decision on any major company decision. Nevertheless, the concept of using such collective group decision making at lower levels within the organization is directly traced to the Hawthorne Studies and in that sense introduced a Western bias in the major industrial, organizational change effort of Japan. The bias was culturally compatible and represented the best that Western managerial thought had to offer.

As described in Chapter 2, apparently some companies abuse the circle with company informers, but the hope is that, since this has become common knowledge to all workers, company leadership will recognize the long-run disadvantages and return to a system of electing group leaders by members of the group instead of appointment by the company. One suspects that the Japanese will quickly correct abuses of the system.

The Ujamaa System

The other example, which was less contaminated in its origin by Western bias (but should have been), is the development and implementation of the Ujamaa system (a rather radical rural organizational change) in Tanzania. The foundation of the system was to move people from existing villages to new Ujamaa villages. The rationale behind regrouping the entire rural population into Ujamaa villages (in a way not unlike the fortified cantons created as a counterinsurgency strategy in Vietnam and Guinea-Bissau) did not make much sense to the Western observer and likewise made little sense to the Tanzanian villager.

Under the Ujamaa organizational plan, the policy decision to move the rural population was based on the following rationale:

1. Better use of available resources to increase production as producers take advantage of economies of scale in productivity, purchasing, and so forth.

2. More efficient use of labor in the rural sector through division of labor and specialization, increased dissemination of agricultural and nonagricultural skills, and increased work discipline.

3. Introduction of a socialist mode of production to check development of class formation as well as tendencies toward human exploitation and excessive differentiation in wealth, income, and power.

4. Broadly based peasant participation in making and implementing decisions that affect their daily lives, hence evolving toward a genuine democracy.[7]

One of the overriding reasons for collectivizing people in such villages was that their original settlements were widely scattered, making the cost of periodic government services somewhat expensive. This is an egregious example of colonial Western bureaucratic thinking. Even worse was the fact that it was promulgated by black men upon other black men. Instead of modifying the program to meet the needs of the citizenry, the people were grossly inconvenienced to suit the needs of the program. The bureaucratic rationale was that people would be provided with better services, a more reliable water supply, and theoretically equivalent pieces of land (as determined by bureaucrats).

It is well known that the Ujamaa system has been less than successful. Even its own originators acknowledge problems with making administrative and technical bureaucrats truly accountable to the people in performance of their development roles. Moreover, they conceded that it was difficult to mediate inherent conflicts between villages, urban and rural interests, and to set priorities.[8] The primary element missing in the Ujamaa system was the kind of training that could produce the administrator and extension personnel who had the management skills to convince people that it was logical to move. This is the Western bias that should have been brought in to increase the chances of success. Begun originally as a voluntary program, in the end it became compulsory and was even more resisted. But, above all, for a program that was designed to promote democracy and participation, apparently very little involvement of the recipient in the design of the system was permitted. Had that very basic tenet of effective organizational change—finding out what the client group and its culture feel about a possible change—been initiated in the first place, it would have been possible to conclude that development of such a system as it was ultimately implemented was inappropriate.

Consequently, it is not necessarily bad to have some Western influence in the development of a major change strategy for it was Westerners who pointed out the lack of logic in this change effort. Sadly, foreigners sometimes have a better idea of what makes a society work than do its own officials. One can equally make the statement about change in the United States—a tradition that goes back to the days of de Toqueville.

WHAT ORGANIZATIONAL CHANGE TECHNIQUES CAN CONTRIBUTE TO THIRD WORLD CHANGE AND DEVELOPMENT

Effectively implemented organizational change efforts can make a contribution to development by putting a reality test upon a proposed change within a given country to make sure that a development idea, such as the Ujamaa system, really should be implemented. One way organizational change techniques are particularly useful is by putting more rigor upon the rationale and cultural analytical process of a given possibility. Analysis also requires the designers to face the hard test of reality rather than muddled wishful, untested, ideologically based thinking. The Japanese did that. The Tanzanians did not.

For example, consider the Ujamaa system again. After a somewhat lack-luster performance, investigators concluded that the reasons for the ineffective performance were:

1. People involved in the project had always worked independently and were un-convinced that communal production would benefit them.

2. Graft and corruption with the reporting of communal income and expenditures lead to general discontent among villagers.

3. In the absence of a means to measure an individual's contribution to communal projects and returns, those who worked felt exploited by those who did not.[9]

A preliminary cultural analysis of the village environment could have eliminated utilizing a communal feature in the development of the new rural development program because it would have required a more rigorous analysis of the preex-isting environment as a prerequisite for the design of the new organizational structure. As presented in Chapter 2, a more logical approach would have been to consult the beneficiaries and get their input before investing in the project. The inclusion of beneficiaries in the design team would have provided further reality testing. As an example of how to go about that, consider utilizing an or-ganizational design approach (such as the one illustrated in Chapter 2) as a means of analyzing and designing the Ujamaa system.

The first effort would be to define the problem and then establish the criteria that both planners and beneficiaries have in mind. To review, criteria are the standards and judgments that planners and recipients use in evaluating a solu-tion. It is furthermore important to determine the differential weight of those criteria since in the final matrix analysis not including those differentials could result in recommending the wrong solution. One would then develop alterna-tives that would best satisfy the defined problem. Instead of restricting oneself to ideological considerations in the development of alternative solutions, a good organizational change effort would also consider alternatives that did not neces-sarily follow the party line. Finally, and most importantly, the evaluators of the solution would be both the people whom the new system would serve as well as the program designers of the organization. This last point cannot be over-emphasized, for using organizational change techniques that stack the deck against the people they should help is no better than using traditional autocratic methods that, in a more blatant manner, stack the deck by not allowing any input by the people the program will serve.

Following this more rigorous analysis procedure, the development of a Ujamaa-like rural development service might have followed a pattern such as the one presented in the following organization design flow chart.

An Organizational Analysis That Accounts for the Effects of Culture and History Upon the Process

Problem

The need to expand agricultural production in the rural areas of African country A. Country A is typified by a gross lack of infrastructure and facilities to help its people, so that any organizational change made will have to maximize the use of the government's resources in such a manner that the maximum number of people will be benefited with the greatest amount of return for the investment.

Client Group

A scattered group of villages consisting of peoples of different language groups, technological practices, and cultural beliefs. Some villages have a centuries-old tradition of hostility toward each other.

Criteria: As Determined by Program Designers from Change Organization A

1. All rural peoples shall be forced to live within commercial villages and forced to work together for the common good.
2. To maximize efficiency, these rural people shall be moved from their original village sites and forced to live in new villages some distance from their homelands.
3. All collective earnings shall be redistributed according to the needs of the specific individuals.
4. Administrative and technical bureaucrats will be truly accountable to the people they are assigned to serve.

Criteria: As Determined by the Beneficiaries and a Specially Trained Design Team from Organization A[10]

1. Based upon an investigation of the cultural beliefs of the villages and specific input from villagers who joined the assessment team, it was found that:
   A. People do not have a tradition of communal agricultural production and would resist efforts to make them live that way.
   B. People are animist and ancestor worshippers by tradition and would resist movement from their homelands, which they view as sacred.
   C. People have a long tradition of personal antagonism toward each other and would resist any redistribution of money they had earned to other villagers.

D. Based upon a long history of exploitation (as well as the current behavior of agricultural extension agents who talk down to them or use technical language they cannot understand), the people do not believe that administrators and technicians would be held accountable to them.

Three Alternative Solutions

1. Ideological: As Determined by Bureaucrats from Change Organization A. Proceed with the development of a program that will force people to move from their homelands to a communal village and way of life.

2. Cultural: As Determined by the Joint Beneficiary—Organization A Team. Develop a rural program that recognizes all the cultural constraints realized in the investigation of the beneficiaries' criteria and that addresses those concerns. This may prove costly because it does not have the infrastructure support advantages that would be obtained through the process of consolidation in communal villages.

3. Compromise: Through further investigation of potential participants, determine what compromises could be made both in the ideological and cultural solutions so that an efficient program could be developed that would be supported by the people it serves. Rely upon those people as colleagues in that process and, in fact, make them members of the design team. Finally after doing the preliminary investigation, quantify the acceptability of each solution through an evaluation process such as the matrix evaluation process described in Chapter 2. For this hypothetical example, an analysis of the first two opposed alternatives is provided.

As indicated in Chapter 2, a weight value of five means that a criterion does not constrain the implementation of a solution, and consequently it will be possible to implement that solution. The largest numerical value means the best solution to the problem.

Using this procedure, the program designers detailed and quantitatively justified the solution below.

Solution Evaluation by Organization A

To develop agriculture adequately in country A, all people will be moved from their traditional homelands to centralized village sites. They will all work for the common good and share their earnings with all of their fellow villagers.

The program designers then compared their solution with their four criteria and produced the following matrix:

	C_1	C_2	C_3	C_4	Total Weight
Solution A	5	5	5	5	20

Finding that the solution matched their criteria perfectly, they felt it was the best solution to improving agriculture in the country. However, the assessment team using the beneficiaries in their assessment process come up with a different solution.

Team Solution and Evaluation by Beneficiary and Organization A

Because potential participants do not have a communal pattern of agricultural production, they resist movement from their homelands, do not like other villages, and distrust the extension staff from the change organization. A decentralized development effort that will serve villages in their present locations through participative village development teams, and will be administered by a new corps of extension agents, will best maximize the chance of improving agricultural production.

The beneficiary design team then compared this solution to their four criteria and produced the following matrix:

	C_1	C_2	C_3	C_4	Total Weight
Solution A	5	5	5	5	20

In this case it was a standoff with the designers all supporting the ideological solution and the villagers all advocating the cultural solution. Both were indifferent to the compromise solution because they had biased their responses to what they believed in the most.

If we wanted to be superbly technical in this analysis, we could to to an interpretive structural modeling analysis of the three solutions and specifically show both sides how they had deliberately biased their responses. That is not really necessary, however, because the discussion during the evaluation process along with the final total scores clearly show that each side biased their analysis and refused to compromise.

The issue ultimately would come to the power base. Clearly, despite the evidence provided by the analysis, one can use the old "do it our way, go along with ideology" and develop a system that from its very beginning will be inappropriate to the clients' needs and thus not be supported. This happened in the Ujamaa case and most recently in the United States where Coca-Cola, despite its market studies, decided that people needed a new Coke only to find that they wanted the old Coke. While not wanting to applaud the behavior of a large transnational company such as Coca-Cola, what they did (which is the final step of this analysis example) was to react immediately to the feedback that they were not successful in marketing the new product and return to producing what customers wanted. In the case of the Ujamaa system, it took a decade before the government would concede that the system failed. The point of a useful organizational change analysis is to get the input of all the participants and draw up a blueprint that will maximize efficiency and satisfaction while minimizing cost and conflict. If analysis cannot pass that test, then it should be thrown out and a new design developed.[11] There are ways to train people, regardless of their education, to be effective in this process. Chapter 6 will suggest some of the specific training exercises that can be used. As an example, the beneficiary-Organization A team, which developed solution 2, would have been trained on how to work cooperatively so a compromise, solution 3, could have been worked out for this problem. Unfortunately, bureaucracy too often is an inhibitor to an effective change—the subject of the next section.

BUREAUCRACY AS AN INHIBITOR TO EFFECTIVE CHANGE

Too often in the developing country setting, despite the negative feedback about the lack of success of a project effort, the organization in charge will continue a fruitless effort trying to get a program to work that in no way matches the constraints of its beneficiaries (unlike a large corporation, which sees losses of sales as losses of profits and reacts immediately to minimize those losses). Public organizations have, in the past, not been particularly worried about that largely because of their bureaucratic focus, which traditionally does not have a quantifiable bottom line such as profits or even concern about the people they serve.

Francis Korten asserts that bureaucratic conflicts occur because

national governments want to centralize control over resources to keep programs responsive to its changing priorities. Hence it sets up on administrative framework to facilitate this objective and expects individual agencies to work within that framework. Yet the individual agency that wishes to pursue a participatory approach needs to allow for greater local control (thus counteracting the government's central control) if it is to be responsive to community interests and decisions.[12]

Of course, there are always forces within the agencies that wish to see central control dominate since local control, as it becomes more effective, eliminates the need for excess bureaucrats. The beneficiaries will take over more of those administrative functions.

The conservatism of agencies whose original mission was to serve a specific group, but becomes more neurotic as demands for participation by beneficiaries increase, is not limited to the Third World. The union movement in the United States has experienced a similar phenomenon in organizations where management has initiated a more participative approach in its operations. Union leaders become more autocratic when they see that their position of authority in handling the affairs of their membership (wage negotiations, grievance settlement, shop steward positions, etc.) can be displaced as workers are increasingly allowed to handle these functions by themselves. Unions have become increasingly resistant to the introduction of participative approaches in U.S. industry. From that perspective, union leadership is really no different than the traditional hierarchical power relationship of management to subordinate. The difference is that autocratic control of union members by unions in the fight against the autocratic control of management supposedly has more redeeming social value—particularly if wages increase.

In the bureaucratic issue of central versus local control, another way to achieve this is to create new autonomous support organizations that would have a specific mandate to foster local control as well as an order to develop a structure that would nurture the participative input of beneficiaries. In theory this would be the best way to go about creating local control. Participation would serve as a countervailing force against central control. This is especially so because one could use all the available organizational design tools to build this ideal structure. For the developing countries, however, there are problems with this strategy. Cost, and the effect upon other national organizations once the autonomous organization is integrated into the national network, are two problems to be discussed in the following section.

AUTONOMY AS A WAY TO CONTROL BUREAUCRACY

One of the classical experiments in using autonomy as a primary mode for organizational change and effectiveness has been the Puebla Project, which operated in the state of Puebla, Mexico, as an autonomous agricultural development program from 1967 to 1975 when it became Plan Puebla and part of the national Mexican agricultural program.

Organized on humanistic lines, the Puebla Project used a special screening process to get young graduates (who rated high on empathy) from the National School of Agriculture as extension agents in the program.[13] These agents were then given additional training in group dynamics and integrated into the existing program, which relied upon transferring technology to small groups of participants in the program.

In addition, a special effort to incorporate farmers into the decision-making process was made. Test plots of corn variations on participant farm landholdings were established. Farmers were invited to the National School of Agriculture to participate in the decision on whether to use national seed varieties or hybrid seed. The final decision was based on growth studies that showed little difference in productivity when a sufficient amount of fertilizer is used. The decision was arrived at rationally and was a direct outcome of farmer participation in the decision-making process.

The autonomy of the organization, moreover, allowed the creation of a participative structure, specialized training for staff within the organization, and adequate supply of logistic and infrastructure support (fertilizer, herbicide, agricultural credit). Unfortunately, when the project reverted to national control, things did not work as well. The best students could not be obtained for the extension jobs (salaries, for example, were established at regular national rates), logistic and equipment support began to fail, and infrastructure supply became sporadic and undependable. The major reason for the turn of events was the loss of subsidy from external funding sources, which was supplied to the project effort during the pilot stage. Consequently, one of the lessons to be learned from the Puebla Project is that if the autonomous structure is to be created it is important to make certain that it will be able to remain autonomous and, secondly, that the sources of funding will remain consistent through time. That, of course, is an ideal state, but in reality it probably would not be possible to get such a guarantee. One only has to look at the budgetary bottlenecks of developmental agencies in the United States to see that long-term commitment is indeed difficult.

The fact that the Puebla Project was able to remain autonomous for eight years with excellent funding and was able to do such an excellent job with its beneficiaries is, in a sense, a monument in itself. Unfortunately, in the case of subsistence farmers who invested in the project and had not accepted the businessman's expectation that there would be dry years, a great deal of scepticism and bitterness was created by the fact that they could not rely upon the continued support of the project. This is not a trait unique to the Third World. The same bitterness occurs when a low-income mother in the United States gets kicked off her infant food supplement program because the government feels that malnourished infants are a better tradeoff in saving a few dollars.

In changing organizations, one must remain aware of the difficulty of carrying out the process. It is true that organizational change techniques can help produce organizations that are effective, productive, and help improve the basic lives of participants in a change program. But there obviously are outside environmental factors that will influence those efforts. Bureaucratic factors, to some extent, are uncontrollable (such as decisions to cut funding of certain programs or, possibly worse, to underfinance them so that one gets a bad job continued through time instead of a clean break and good memories). It is a reality that will not change as we slide into the twenty-first century, for most likely change will still remain dependent upon bureaucracy and politics.

There were, however, two outstanding achievements of the Puebla Project. It showed that an agricultural development mission could be effectively organized in terms of small groups and that beneficiaries could effectively interact with administrators in the planning and decision-making aspects of a change program. It showed that elements of the beneficiaries' culture could be incorporated in designing more effective organizations. The second major achievement was the introduction of training management and personnel to a cultural sensitivity of the beneficiaries they serve. Extension staff as well as administrators received instruction upon the cultural differences between them and the beneficiaries. But above all the autonomy of the organization played the significant role in the development of the project and its initial success. Without that autonomy, it is doubtful that the experiments in participation, group decision making, and attention to the cultural difference of the participants would have occurred. Mexican agricultural programs in the traditional mode are highly autocratic.

The ultimate issue is autonomy versus reformation. Autonomy of an organization works because it does not have a load of behavioral baggage to correct (the past misdeeds of the organization members). Reformation is a time-consuming and difficult process. As described in Chapter 1, with the organization change example, there is a good chance that even long-term efforts at reformation will fail. Most countries will proceed with a mixture of both strategies, namely, building new autonomous organizations when it is feasible and making efforts to reform existing organizations that cannot, for whatever reason, be terminated. It is hoped that the best of Western culture as well as the host-country culture will be incorporated in the design of either effort.

THE EFFECTIVE INITIATION OF ORGANIZATIONAL CHANGE IN A DEVELOPING COUNTRY

Not surprisingly, the effective initiation of organizational change depends upon the kind and quality of people responsible for the changes made within the person's home organization. The origin of the initiation of the process can be both internal and external. Focusing on the external first, there are two ways to initiate organizational change. One way is indirect, through international educational programs (be they Soviet or capitalist inspired). Certainly this writer has trained enough Latin American, Iranian, and African students to hope that all the training they got on participation, group decision making, and organization development will be applied once they return to their homelands. Consequently, this indirect external approach could become an internal force as administrators within their organizations try a more democratic method when changing their organizations. The logic is that my students and other similarly trained students will be there to help.

One of the strategies that has received the most professional attention in the past several years is the external training of people from developing countries in out-of-country short-term programs on management techniques. While such efforts may not focus fully on organizational change, they certainly introduce some of the elements of organizational change that under the right leadership could be a positive force for change within the host-country institutions that those people return to.

The reader may not be aware of some of the simplest management skills that many of these external training courses provide. For example, in such training programs there are people who have never thought of defining objectives before planning a project, and who have never considered using a relatively simple evaluation process such as a matrix evaluation—let alone of using groups as a vehicle for group decision making. Few such people, on their own, would consider including in the planning process the people to be actually affected by a new program.

This, however, is not meant to be all that critical for I recently had the same experience while consulting for a large local organization involved in a long-term planning project. I found that managers viewed specifying one's objectives, criteria, and project evaluation technique as somewhat of a revelation.

The focus of Chapter 4 will be to discuss in greater detail some of the past and present external training programs and to provide more detail on the advantages and disadvantages of the internal and external organizational change initiation process. As such, this section has served as a brief introduction to that subject.

SUMMARY

Cultural bias is an inherent problem in the organizational change process. It comes both from the culture of the Third World country that is in the process of change and from the international agencies that offer help in effecting organizational change.

One of the factors in cultural bias is the history of a particular country. Many countries have a long history of exploiting a specific group, as in the case of the Indians of Bolivia. Other countries, such as Tanzania, have a colonial history, which in the professional behavior of its change agents can result in nationals taking on the behavioral characteristics of their former masters and behaving in an ineffective neocolonial manner. It is necessary for the developmental organization to examine how history has affected culture and how that bias, in turn, affects its current operations.

When a Third World change agency works with an international organization, there is always the possibility that a Western bias will be introduced into the change process. Such a bias, however, has both positive and negative possibilities. Optimally, the best of both organizations should be incorporated into the design of the organizational change.

To illustrate advantages and disadvantages of the Western influence, two case examples were detailed: Japanese industrialization and the Ujamaa system in Tanzania. Japan accepted the best the West had to offer and excelled in its industrial development. Tanzania accepted the worst tenets of colonial thinking and correspondingly failed miserably in its major rural development change effort. The point to be made in these examples is that by eliminating ideology, and introducing participation and involvement of beneficiaries in the design process of organizational change, one has a somewhat better chance of achieving success. To illustrate that point, a section was included to show how assessment teams can evaluate a design effort and to demonstrate the role that culture and power play in that process.

Two kinds of organizational development are most often proposed: the development of autonomous organizations and the reformation of existing organizations. Autonomous organizations have the advantage of controlling cultural bias because they are free to move in whatever direction they wish with only limited strings attached. The Puebla Project illustrated how cultural understanding can be used to effect a viable organizational structure. On the other hand, reformation is a difficult process because of the lack of control the change organization has. In reforming such an organization, one must deal with the cultural bias(es) of the existing bureaucracy and power structure. It is a difficult process that often fails, but it is the path that organizational change must most often follow, for the development of autonomous organizations is more an anomaly than a commonality.

Cultural bias in Third World organizational change will continue to be an inhibiting factor for the foreseeable future. It is not, however, an insurmountable barrier. With the right kind of people, cultural bias can even be a force that will promote the effectiveness of organizational change efforts. The crux, however, is the training and development of those people. Forthcoming chapters will discuss the nature and process of producing people who not only will understand the inherent effects of culture in the change process but will be able to utilize that reality in initiating change efforts in their respective organizations.

NOTES

1. Gwynne Dyer, *WAR* (New York: Crown, 1985).

2. International Development Bank Newsletter, September 1985.

3. Gene Erb, "Cheap Mexican Labor Drains Jobs from Iowa," *Des Moines Register,* March 16, 1986, p. 1C.

4. Francis Korten, "Community Participation: A Management Perspective on Obstacles and Options," in *Bureaucracy and the Poor,* ed. David C. Korten and Felipe B. Alfonso, (New York: McGraw-Hlll, 1981), p. 199.

5. Justin Maeda, "Creating National Structures for People Centered Agrarian Development," in *Bureaucracy and the Poor,* ed. David C. Foster and Felipe B. Alfonso, (New York: McGraw-Hill, 1981), p. 140.

6. Ibid., p. 145.

7. Ibid., p. 148.

8. Ibid., p. 150.

9. Ibid., p. 146.

10. The specially trained design team could have undergone a special group analysis training, as explained in Chapter 6.

11. Allen Jedlicka, "Mini-Corporate Cultures and Regional Economic Development," paper presented at the Conference of the American Association for the Advancement of Science, May 1986, Philadelphia.

12. Korten, "Community Participation," p. 198.

13. Allen Jedlicka, *Organization for Rural Development* (New York: Praeger, 1977).

4

Initiating Organizational Change Efforts

The government said we could only sell our cattle at government determined prices. And that's all right for now we run our cattle to Senegal in the evening and get paid with real money—French Francs.

Fulani Tribesman

INTRODUCTION

One of the first things the Guinea-Bissau government did after winning its colonial war with Portugal was to make a unilateral change in its market system to that of a centrally determined price structure based on the Soviet model.[1] The immediate result was a major food shortage since farmers could easily run their produce to neighboring Senegal where there is a demand for their products. Obviously, in this unplanned change effort, the government made the mistake of assuming that farmers would respond positively to selling their products at a loss.

A great deal has been written on the subject of how one goes about effectively initiating a change effort. In Chapter 2, some classical examples of how that change process is analyzed and developed were presented with the admonition that even in its Western home of origin the process is still somewhat lacking and that appropriate modifications are needed to use existing techniques effectively in a Third World environment.

One of the central questions is whether an internal or external process is better. There are advantages and disadvantages to both, and it would be better not to try to categorize one or the other as superior, but take the contingency or theory Z view that, subject to a given environment, one or the other approach or a hybrid mixture of both (given an appropriate organizational assessment) will produce an appropriate change strategy.

While on the surface the contingency approach may seem a cop-out, in reality it has been a breakthrough in organizational change thinking. No longer are designers required to stick to the orthodoxy of a specific theoretical approach; instead, they are given the planning freedom to utilize whatever is useful to a given environmental situation.

But considering the original dichotomy of external versus internal processes, conventional wisdom indicates that reliance upon external strategies allows an organization to utilize the skills of international experts who bring their expertise to the fold in developing a change strategy. A major problem has always been that too often such experts are motivated primarily by the retainer they receive, that too often such experts are not really experts at all, but individuals (often with dubious skills and reputation) who have been dragged up to fulfill a contract. Finally, even in the best circumstances, very competent people may not be contracted long enough to get an effective understanding of all the cultural nuances that bear upon the effective design of organizational changes.

When one looks at internal efforts, one runs into the mirror image of the external approach. While cultural knowledge of the environment probably exists, the skills in designing organizational changes are often lacking (although with the impact of a new generation of managers trained in behavioral skills this variable is becoming more and more controlled). Thus, theoretically a blend of both strategies may serve as the best means of designing effective organizational changes. This chapter, then, will analyze the effects of external versus internal change efforts, hybrid forms, and the role that international business can play in serving as a complementary external change agent. Some case examples of external, internal, and hybrid change strategies will then be provided.

INITIATION OF CHANGE STRATEGIES—WESTERN BLOC VERSUS EASTERN BLOC COUNTRIES

Too often, an assumption in books on development that originate in the Western countries is that it is only the West that is trying to introduce organizational change within the developing countries. In fact, the Eastern bloc countries are also engaged in that process and, when they are allowed to enter a country, have some very effective, power-based methods of effecting those changes. They use techniques that Western countries are not ideologically committed to, although one of the techniques, operant conditioning, is used by both sides and can be viewed as a tool for good or evil depending on which side of the fence one stands.

As an example, consider the current occupation (or liberation, depending on one's ideology) of Afghanistan by the Soviet Union. According to our news sources, this Muslim country is now experiencing the evacuation of many of its children to the Soviet Union where a new generation of Afghan children will be carefully schooled in Marxist ideology and belief in the Soviet Union. They ultimately will be returned to the country to serve as the new ruling generation.

While one does not envision a draconion reinforcement of proper behavior of these children (such as illustrated in the futuristic society of *A Clockwork Orange*), one can be sure that positive reinforcement (both verbal and substantive, such as monetary and special privilege rewards) is being used in that training so that the returning cadre will be true believers. Unfortunately, just as it works in the case of U.S. families turning their children into good democrats or fundamentalists, it will work there.

Since Afghans are a culturally unique group of people, one would like to believe that the effort will be a failure, similar to Mormon efforts to reculturate Zuni Indians from their own tribal religion to that of Mormonism (by providing free education in Utah to volunteers). The Zunis were very pragmatic in their rationale for allowing their children to participate. As they said, "you Anglos and the Catholic church have spent 400 years trying to change us and failed—Mormons are no different. Meanwhile, our kids get one hell of an education."[2]

In the Afghan case, the major difference will be that once the children return they will not go back to the fold of their family for deprogramming. At the current scale of village attrition, those parents are either already or soon will be dead. But it is amazing how resilient cultural change can be, and the U.S. Bureau of Indian Affairs (BIA) stands out as another example of long-term failure to change one cultural group into another. The verdict is still out on how successful Soviet efforts will be (no doubt they have studied the BIA training manual on reculturation) in effecting organizational change within Afghanistan through the institution of a cadre of conditioned children. We Westerners want to believe that we can initiate effective change without using the brute force of the Soviet model.

THE WESTERN EXTERNAL INITIATIVE APPROACH

Those of us from the Western countries like to view ourselves as the good guys (no doubt the Soviets view themselves likewise) and try to overlook the effects that, in many countries, the former colonial system, which only rather recently ended, may have upon a country's degree of enthusiasm to work with us. The British, in the nineteenth century, really behaved no differently than the Soviets do today.

But that is probably a minor effect, for by and large the Third World specifically invites international agencies and First World government organizations to help participate in the great adventure of development (anomalies such as Grenada and Nicaragua do occur, although, at this writing, I do not believe large numbers of Grenadian children are being educated in Newark to be good little democrats—God forbid that should happen, given the type of product a big U.S. city school system produces).

There are, nevertheless, a number of agencies within First World democratic governments that focus on training Third World functionaries in the mechanics and process of organizational change. A few of those efforts will be presented in the next section of the chapter.

ADVANTAGES AND DISADVANTAGES OF THE EXTERNAL AND INTERNAL STRATEGIES

There are some advantages as well as disadvantages in both the external and internal initiation of change strategies. In the case of external initiation, there is always a price to be paid if one lets the outsider do it.

One of the prices to be paid if external initiation comes from the United States is the amount of payment the host country will have to make in paperwork and labor that produces that help. If the United States is going to be involved, it will expect a proposal that will have to be written in a way that satisfies the personal needs of the bureaucrats who will review and assess the worthiness of the proposal.

Obviously that is not asking all that much because, if a country does want the involvement of the external agency, it should be prepared to show good faith and write down what that agency expects to hear. The problem with many small countries is that there are so few talented people who are able, after the cultural debugging of these assignments occurs, to write and manage the paper-pushing part of the job. Yet another problem is that there are not many qualified people, after that step is completed, actually to get involved in the job that the proposal addresses.

A far more significant problem is that relying upon the external source introduces a certain degree of bias in whatever is developed, because inevitably it means the introduction of expatriate professionals who may or may not have the best interests of the country in mind. There is, after all, a certain element of international professionals who, while they do a professional job, can also do a professional job that is irrelevant to the particular needs of the organization and the country it serves.

On the other side of the fence, one might expect that the use of an internal initiation process may be more effective because the internal sources are in a better position to know what is needed within the organization. However, that is not necessarily true. For example, I worked for some years as an organizational change consultant to another international organization. While my section leader more or less had the same professional skills as I did, his mission was survival because he had to spend, as he put it, some 90 percent of his time protecting his back. Consequently, I did the work while he played bodyguard. Obviously, this is an expensive strategy since it requires two people to do the work that one should have been able to do if the internal environment were safer. The irony was that the agency was in the business of initiating organizational change in other organizations (which had similar degrees of mistrust and downright hostility as existed in this agency) yet had no effective way of initiating organizational changes within its own environment.

Solomon and Heegard have studied the dilemma of limited labor (and the effects of internal versus external initiation strategies) and have suggested the following approaches. In their paradigm three alternatives are available to the organization wishing to initiate a change process.[3]

The first alternative is basically an expatriate model where an expatriate team of professionals is brought into an organization and single-handedly runs the organization. Many of the former colonies in Africa have relied upon this approach and, in the early days of national freedom, often hired the people who worked there when it was still under control of the former colonial power.

Properly utilized expatriates who are trained in the belief that their function is, as with any good change agent, to do the job well and then get out can be an effective mode; however, when relying solely on expatriates, a certain degree of dependency, at best, will be established that can inhibit the development of indigenous control.

The second alternative, known as the indigenous model, is more productive, at least for creating an indigenous capability. In this approach, the expatriates would be under the control of an indigenous coordinator who would have formal responsibility for the mission of the change of organization.

Because of the element of being able to control what is being done, better understanding of the unique environment of the organization, and direct relevance to achieving organizational objectives, an internal initiation process is preferable to that of reliance upon expatriates (when there are enough trained people who understand the techniques involved). Expatriates, after all, are expensive and probably temporary at best.

The problem is that most countries often just do not have a sufficient number of properly trained people to do the job. There have been efforts by a number of countries to produce that kind of person with the specific intention that they remain within their own countries after receiving training. That is, rather than training young people in U.S. universities (which runs the risk that they will become part of the brain-drain problem and remain within the States), short courses are provided to selected personnel either in their own country or in brief training sessions in the sponsoring country. While these people are taught by expatriate consultants, the specific strategy is that they return to their respective countries and become indigenous change agents and trainers who do not rely upon the support of an in-country expatriate team of consultants. This last approach of Solomon and Heegard is commonly recognized as the best long-term alternative. It is fraught with the problems of turnover and commitment by top management of the Third World organization, but it is a strategy that through repetition can produce a sufficient number of skilled personnel and eliminate dependence on expatriates. Crucial to such a strategy is the appropriate training of indigenous personnel, which is the subject of the following section.

PROPER TRAINING OF INDIGENOUS PERSONNEL

Agencies such as USDA, World Bank, and the Organization of American States in varying degrees have all been involved in some sort of organizational change training. Depending upon the core of specialists who develop the specific guidelines for training programs, there is usually concern for communicating the importance of small-group development in the change process. A common way of illustrating that importance is by requiring participants to function as small groups during the actual training sessions. The rationale behind such approaches is that if the trainees are to return to their home organizations and try to apply some of the small-group techniques they have been taught, it is better to have at least some experience in functioning as group members during the training phase.

In education such an approach is called experiential learning. The rationale is that those who experience a technique will have a greater chance of retaining and understanding the information acquired during the training process. Studies show that after a year most people will still retain as much as 40 percent of the information acquired under experiential learning but only 10 percent of the information acquired under a traditional lecture format. Yet, all too often, training programs still rely upon a heavy dose of stultifying lectures as the core of a program's learning process.

A primary concern is to attempt to change (if only on the surface) existing attitudes that members of the organization bring with them (of course, in Chapter 2 the difficulties in accomplishing that were outlined). The most common attitude one finds in trainees is a strong belief that autocratic authority is the best way to do things. In a training effort, even for programs that do not effect a total attitude change as a baseline (as one would in a training program having more emphasis on psychological change) it is nevertheless necessary to force participants to recognize that some individual attitude adjustment, even if it is not total, is necessary to make things work. In essence, this is falling back on a modified psychological change idea that old attitudes can be partially unfrozen, with new ones recognized and accepted into a new pattern of behavior. The more rigorous Lewin requirement of totally unfreezing old attitudes and refreezing new attitudes is not used in this approach.[4]

Realists among us know that most people do not become total converts, but we also know that they can become workable skeptics without making a total personality change—perhaps that is all one should really expect. The limited use of administrative power in this process is also acceptable. If top managers do not make it evident that they wish to see changes in behavior in a certain direction, then most likely they will not occur. There are, regardless, some people who will not change, and they will have to be put in a position of least damage to the organization.

The kind of background training for indigenous personnel, then, would focus on the understanding of the value of small-group process, a participative management style, and the need for client involvement in the decision making of the change organization as outlined in Chapter 2. A major problem, however, with much of the international training provided is that it concentrates on internal control, teaching techniques such as cost-benefit analysis, critical-path analysis, and a host of planning and scheduling techniques outlined in the notes section of Chapter 2. Such training makes nice bureaucrats, but it does not produce humanistic change agents.

One reason for having such an international training emphasis is that it is politically safe. Military-controlled countries, for example, do not mind having their people learn about internal control techniques. After all, it is probably useful for consolidating their power. But when you talk seriously about such things as equal participation, involvement of the beneficiaries in the design of changing governmental agencies, and the need of a national policy to support a more open society, you are talking about serious matters that some governments may object to. Consequently, too often international agencies take the safe route in training and then lament in later decades why a regime such as Marcos's could dominate a country for so long. Part of the answer is that international training efforts too often, by taking the easy route, support such governments de facto. Consequently, they produce "change agents" who could not care less about being agents of change, but who get damn good at processing a PERT chart or cost-benefit analysis.

LONG-TERM OBJECTIVES OF CHANGING THE CHANGE AGENTS

The argument that must be accepted for long-term effects in creating effective change agents is similar to Dyer's statements about the development of a truly international community (which in essence is the core of this book).

As for the argument that there will never be universal brotherhood among mankind, and so any attempt to move beyond the current system of national states [substitute autocratic behavior in organizations] is foredoomed: of course we aren't going to end up loving one another indiscriminately, but that isn't necessary. There is not universal love and brotherhood within national states either. What does exist, and what must be extended beyond national borders, is a mutual recognition that everybody is better off if they respect each others' rights and accept arbitration by a higher authority rather than shooting each other when their rights come into conflict.[5]

Similarly, the purpose of training within the organization is to get people to respect others' rights and use a democratic means of addressing concerns instead of brute power by whomever has it. It will not create universal brotherhood in this generation, but if it continues from a baseline of reformed autocrats and concerned people, some generation in the future may actually be able to produce that universal brotherhood.

Exercises that can be used in training people to achieve those long-term objectives are the primary concern of Chapter 6. Consequently, discussion of specific training techniques is reserved for that chapter.

EFFECTIVE MANAGEMENT

A strong case has been made in Chapter 2 for the use of small groups and participative organizational structures as a primary means of effecting organizational change and designs for the twenty-first century. Implicit in all this is the training of managers who can make these kinds of systems work. Autocrats, it has been suggested, do not match our objectives all that well.

One of the ways by which managers can be more effective is through the use of positive reinforcement, or operant conditioning, in their interpersonal relationships with staff and beneficiaries. This section will discuss the relevance of operant conditioning to the internal development of managers who can effectively deal with organizational change.

OPERANT CONDITIONING: RELEVANCY TO TWENTY-FIRST CENTURY ORGANIZATIONAL DESIGN

In essence, operant conditioning is the process of using praise, recognition, and incentives to reward an employee for doing a job well. Based on positive reinforcement studies in the 1930s (most often credited to B. F. Skinner) with animals (where the reinforcers typically are food rewards for doing a job correctly), humans are positively reinforced by praise, public recognition, and so on for doing a job well. The research shows that such reinforcement virtually reassures that a job once done well will be repeated in the future. To insure proper repetition of a job, the reinforcement should be given on a sporadic basis. The rationale for that scheduling is that too much of a good thing breeds either casualness or contempt. For example, suppose you were in a program to maximize efficient electricity consumption, and one of the reinforcers was to praise an employee when he shut the lights off before leaving a room. It would work as a reinforcer if the administrator praised the employee on the first, fourth, and eighth day or any other random sequence. It would act as an overworked irritant if the administrator praised the same action ten times a day, ten days in a row.[6]

Incidentally, the classic reinforcer for repetitive human behavior is the slot machine. It does not reinforce a player by continuous reinforcement (that would break the house), but by intermittently scheduled reinforcement—enough to keep you playing, but also in a pattern that benefits the house. This brings us to one of the primary criticisms of operant conditioning—that it is manipulative, a form of subconscious motivation that may make people do things they normally would not do. A lot of this criticism probably came from B. F. Skinner's book *Walden II*, which described how a futuristic society free of the interpersonal failings of contemporary society could be created through operant conditioning. The fear was that people could be conditioned to do things that are immoral or even criminal. The fears are really quite overrated. While it is one thing to get people to improve their performance by praising, a more immoral effort, such as using praise to get a person to beat up a company slacker, just cannot be done. Response to praise is human nature. As children, we all responded to the praise of our parents, and in the business world the situation is really no different. Another more basic way to explain it is by the Golden Rule. Praise others for a good job, and they will continue to do well. Criticize others for a mediocre job, and they will resent you and probably do less. The Old Testament somewhat predates B. F. Skinner.

OPERANT CONDITIONING AND THE CHANGE PROCESS

One thing that is certain, when an organizational change is carried out (whether internally or externally initiated), is that there will be a good deal of stress. If there is no stress, then the job is not being done right. It behooves good managers to use every tool possible to manage the stress. Operant conditioning can help that process. Instead of ignoring or berating employees for mediocre or confused behavior, one could praise the employee for trying and, if performance is good, praise the employee for that work. The classic example of this kind of behavior was a productivity effort by J. F. Feeney in the early 1970s.[7]

Feeney worked as vice-president of systems performance at Emery Air Freight at the time he initiated a Skinnerian approach to resolving a problem of sloppy operations in loading and shipping air freight containers. Managers assumed that large containers were being used 90 percent of the time as dictated by company policy. When Feeney checked the utilization rate, however, he found a figure closer to 45 percent. The solution to get the usage rate up was first to "tell the workers how much they were falling short of the 90 percent utilization rate and how profits would be increased if containers were used at an optimum level."[8] Along with that feedback, checklists were utilized by the workers to show whether 90 percent utilization had been achieved each day so a constant, quantitative measure was available rather than an assumption that the work had been done. The key, however, to the success of this rather mundane organizational change was that the managers were trained to provide very simple verbal reinforcers to the workers when they achieved the utilization rate. Verbal reinforcers were very simple positive statements of fact such as, "John, I'm pleased to see that you have achieved the utilization rate," as well as more generalized positive comments about the employee's overall work performance (in accordance with Skinnerian theory, punishment for poor performance was avoided). The approach is simple because the actual reinforcement is a short compliment. It is difficult because it requires managers, manager trainees, really to believe that positive statements can affect worker behavior.

One then basically has to look at the personal styles of the managers involved in the use of such a program. If an organization is characterized by autocratic managers who have a known, long-term history of autocratic behavior, then it more likely is not going to work when suddenly a very irascible manager starts complimenting his subordinates. For example, imagine that Don Rickles were a manager and had been instructed to begin using positive reinforcement on his employees. Workers would rightly be suspicious of his motivation. But even Don Rickles could change his behavior given time, provided he really wanted to.

Autocratic managers can be trained to change their behavior without going into a lengthy psychoanalysis through a Skinnerian behavior-modification approach. Just as with the program developed by Feeney, autocrats can be given direct feedback about this behavior upon employees and then be trained on how they can modify that behavior in their dealings with other employees. One must realize, as stated earlier, that there are some people who, regardless of what one does, will not change. In that case, the best is to put such people in places where they are harmless.

The primary point to be made is that operant conditioning/positive reinforcement can be an effective tool in dealing with both fellow employees and beneficiaries. In the context of dealing with the process of change, which by definition means conflict, even a little island of positive feedback can help smooth the process. It is a technique that anyone who really cares can learn. Certainly, when handled properly, it provides a useful alternative to the use of autocratic behavior in initiating either internal or external change efforts. The ultimate point is that if effective changes are to be made they will have to be made from a participative theoretical base. Operant conditioning fits well in a participative approach, while autocratic behavior does not. The following section will discuss the nature of autocratic behavior in Third World change organizations and provide case examples of the effect of such behavior.

AUTOCRATIC ADMINISTRATIVE BEHAVIOR IN THE CHANGE PROCESS

Autocracy is unfortunately a still too common behavior in Third World change organizations. It can come from the underlying cultural realities of caste or class, but, whatever the origins, it is one of the major barriers to organizational change in the Third World (and, for that matter, of the United States). As described in one of my earlier writings, autocratic behavior was probably best conceptualized by McGregor in his Theory X and Theory Y topologies.

The Theory X administrator is considered to have a rather primitive or misanthropic conception of human behavior based on the belief that the average man is by nature indolent, resists any change, lacks ambition, and is additionally rather gullible and stupid. Consequently, managers must take all responsibility for organizing, decision-making, supervising, and planning.[9]

The assumption that position makes right, independent of ability, is classic nineteenth century thinking, based upon the early writings of Frederick Taylor and classical, scientific management. It works reasonably well if one has great control over the recipients of that behavior, but it does not promote creativity or enthusiasm toward a job. In the case of trying to get someone to do something that you want done but have no control over, it more often guarantees that nothing will get done. Even autocracy under extreme control is overrated. The extreme example in the United States was the slavery system where it was no accident that a very primitive field worker technology (hoes and shovels) was utilized. Field hands had little incentive to operate more complicated technology; thus, "dumb field hands" who could not grasp more complicated technology were not all that dumb—they would have been fools to make their condition even more demanding.

So when one talks about the need for utilizing such techniques as operant conditioning to implement organizational change, one is also talking about the need for a more flexible, humanistic management view of human behavior. McGregor's Theory Y, now over 40 years old, still best describes the kind of management thinking one must create for an effective organizational change. Some of his views are presented below:

1. People are not by nature passive or resistant to interaction and decision making within organizations. They become so as a result of experience within organization.

2. The motivation, potential for development, capacity for assuming responsibility, and readiness to direct behavior toward organizational involvement are all present in people.

3. The essential task of management is to arrange organizational conditions and methods of operation so that people can achieve their own goals best by directing their own efforts toward achieving organizational objectives.[10]

Unfortunately, to reach that state of understanding or attitude toward other organizational members (if it does not already exist as a natural state) may require an extensive retraining via the subconscious change approach (more or less in line with Kurt Lewin's use of T-groups to unfreeze old attitudes and refreeze new attitudes about a different group of people or the clients one is supposed to serve). It was shown in Chapter 2 that the Third World does not have enough time or capacity to carry out such a task.

The point that has to be made so that this book will not be regarded as a Panglossian adventure is that organizational change and management training are very difficult objectives to achieve. The rate in making successful change efforts has not been very good, and in fact because of the political nature of too many Third World organizations, it may not be possible. The reality may be that the majority of Third World organizations cannot be changed to a more participative structure. If so, we should not be too critical of the Third World since that is basically the same record for First World organizations. However, even if autocracy is too powerful a force to conquer, it is possible to lessen some of the more severe effects of autocracy on employee behavior through training.

EXAMPLES OF INTERNAL ORGANIZATIONAL CHANGE

Some people would say that the only effective organizational change is to create new autonomous organizations and then select and train members to fit the objectives of those organizations. In that way the effects of autocracy can be controlled and the use of techniques such as operant conditioning initiated. This is basically what was accomplished by the Puebla Project (one of the most studied early, participative, rural development programs in the Third World). Management recognized early that reliance upon Mexican national support organizations, stuck in their inefficient, autocratic (and, to a large extent, corrupt) mode of conduct with beneficiaries would not work. In essence, management created its own autonomous developmental agency with the help of Rockefeller and Ford Foundation funding. To control the potential autocratic nature of its administrative staff, special measures were taken to recruit a group of young graduates from the National School of Agriculture who scored high not only on technical ability but in psychological tests on empathy with the beneficiaries they would serve.

The Puebla Project was a relative success up until the mid-1970s where circumstances such as the oil crisis, which affected its reliance upon synthetic fertilizer, immensely impeded its operations (fertilizer, if it were available, became too expensive to buy). But overall its structure, underlying philosophy, and mode of participative group operation were successful. However, that does not mean that the development of new organizations will always result in a participative beneficiary-oriented organization.

While working in Guinea-Bissau on a rice development project (Bissau had recently liberated itself from Portugal), I was able to observe the start-up process of the new government's rural development agencies. There was a chance to create new autonomous organizations free of the hamstrings of political control and able to work participatively with farmers in the field. What farmers got instead was a handful of politicos who literally went around carrying Mao's little red book (even China had given up on that by then) and providing very dull lectures on the evils of capitalism. These people knew very little about rural development, management training, organizational development, or even the cultures of their beneficiaries since, just like us, they needed translators to convert languages like Balanta and Fula into Portuguese Creole. The absurd policy decision of focusing on politicizing the rural proletariat resulted in extreme food shortages as indigenous farmers quickly shipped their produce to Senegal. A coup took place on my last day there that was supposedly at least somewhat pro-Western. A hope by the international community was that the political dogma would be replaced by serious efforts to change the country's development agencies. One predicts a long and difficult transition in the country from colony to country.

Unfortunately, opportunities for effective organizational change through the influence of political dogma can still be nullified. Someone must have written the same thing about events in 1921 when the Bolsheviks in Russia consolidated their power and let incompetents such as Lysenko dominate the change process (Lysenko's theory of acquired characteristics set back Russian agriculture, and rural development stagnated until the late 1960s). Most certainly, from a historical standpoint, the Russian change process was improperly managed, as is the Bissauan.

THE NEED FOR PROPER MANAGEMENT AFTER THE CHANGE PROCESS HAS BEEN INITIATED

The final payoff of the change process (whether from the creation of new organizations or the reformation of existing organizations) is the creation of a body of managers and service personnel (extension staff) who are integrated in their thinking of how to carry out their work with beneficiaries. They will need to know how to use the benefits of small-group development and involve beneficiaries in the design and decision-making processes and how to manage properly both the internal change process within their home organization and in the field.

That, of course, all depends upon how well the training and conversion process is carried out, which will be examined in Chapter 6. Not every effort is successful and the effects of a shoddily implemented change effort can have negative effects in the field. In the following section, two examples of field efforts from an organization that had undergone an internal change in the behavioral style of its managers are provided to illustrate how insufficient training and improper management of the process can lead to problems in the field.

CASE EXAMPLES OF SUCCESS AND FAILURE IN EFFECTING CHANGE

These two examples of organizational change efforts at the village level in Central America illustrate both the best and the worst that can occur during the transition stage of changing the mode of operation of an organization. In these rural development efforts, two villages were to have their economic base expanded by introducing small-business activities. Despite the fact that the same agency worked with the two villages, the outcomes were entirely different due to the environmental circumstances (leadership in the communities) of each village and the managerial capabilities of the project managers of the change organization.

Both villages were located in the same province and in fact were within 20 miles of each other. Both were desperately poor in local resources. Soil erosion in that part of the world is so extreme that only subsoil remains. Farming consists of chopping small holes in the subsoil and planting seed with a small amount of natural or synthetic fertilizer (if either is available).

The initiation process of getting the projects started was through a combination of both internal and external promotion. That is, the international organization that ultimately worked with both villages had a mission to help. At the same time, representatives of the villages came to the organization asking for assistance. A preliminary assessment was made, and based on that assessment it was decided that village A would produce a biscuit product made from a local cheese (the primary economy being livestock production), and village B would produce a canned fruit product (using local produce) that would rely upon labor-intensive canning processes. The objectives were sound because both products were in demand both in the cities and locally. The consequent factory organization and training to carry out those objectives resulted in village A failing and village B succeeding.

Village A did not really have any training in managing the production of the new product. The project manager from the organization essentially agreed to subsidize the raw materials going into the product as well as buy any excess product that could not be sold. However, no specific village-level project manager was selected and trained. Despite management training in participative approaches, the project manager from the organization behaved with a traditional, autocratic managerial style, and there was no community involvement in the design of the system. Production was done by individuals who would make the biscuits and deliver the finished product to the visiting field representative when he came to the village. In short, there was no substantive training of village participants, no responsibility delegated to the villagers, and no way to manage the project once it was initiated.

One can probably guess what happened. Very quickly producers began cutting back on the amount of shortening and cheese in the product, which had all the appeal of hardtack. But since the organization agreed to buy the unsold product (which in short order was all of it since the inedible product could not be sold), the village continued to produce the product, making an additional windfall profit from cutting back on ingredients in the final product.

Producers were amazingly candid, saying such things as, "Well, if they're fools enough to buy this stuff, why not continue to make it."[11] The project ultimately was stopped after a few halfhearted efforts to try to get the participants to behave properly. One, after all, should not romanticize the nobility of villagers. Most of them are just as willing to cheat and cut corners as any business person. It is just that, because they do not control the power to do so, they seldom get the chance.

The key elements of the failure of the project were that the project manager did not do his job properly and no quality control was initiated, but even more importantly, the villagers were not really all that involved in the design and decision-making aspects of the change. To them it seemed to be a turkey ripe for plucking, a short-term operation whose only real function was to be taken.

Village B went a different route. Instead of just dropping a turn-key operation upon villagers, discussion groups were established to determine a range of possibilities that the village might operationalize. Out of those deliberations came the decision to try fruit processing because the area had an abundance of supply. During this discussion a natural village project manager arose and became the formally designated manager. When it came time to select the kind of technology to be used, group discussion was once again used as the decision-making mechanism. Working through that process, the group planning and decision-making efforts were the basis for organizational changes that would have to be made within the village to support the new industry (changes such as establishing a reliable supply of firewood for heat processing, developing a water system for the plant, drawing up a simple accounting system to keep track of fruit supply, and determining costs for purchasing fruit).

The result, in contrast to village A, was a considerable investment of time, money, and organizational change carried out by the villagers, which was supervised and managed by the project manager, who resolved conflicts as they arose. The project effort in this village was a success, but then again it should have been because of the members' investment of group effort and the monitoring and facilitating of the indigenous project manager.

Upon analysis of the two projects, the major problem was that while extensive efforts, in conjunction with experts from outside the country, had been made to change the thinking and practices of the managers in the central organization, that reformation process had not extended to the extension staff. They had not been properly retrained (or replaced) in the techniques of promoting community development and participative involvement of people in the process of change.

In one case, this led to a virtually complete failure of project efforts because properly trained extension staff were not available. The other case was successful because a natural-born leader in the community took over the project manager role and on her own knew how to manage the process once it had been initiated. She was able to do this through her own experience and intuitive understanding of how to get people to work together. The major point is that the organization's failure to train all of its personnel in the new procedures resulted in one failure, while the successful case was only a matter of luck.

THE ROLE OF EXTENSION IN DEVELOPMENT

In an earlier book, *Organization for Rural Development*, I commented extensively on the role of extension agents in the development process, pointing out that they need to be effective in interpersonal communication and group dynamics and also need to be empathetic with and credible to the clients they serve. It is still as true today as it was when the book was written that in the selection and training of extension agents,

the change agency must be aware that these people bear the greatest burden . . . for they are the representatives of the agency that will be most in contact with clients in the field.

If they have not been adequately trained to understand the psychological motivation and needs of their clients, if they do not understand the behavioral antecedents associated with developing groups . . . then one can expect that success in the transfer of a program . . . will be severely handicapped. The importance of controlling this very human . . . variable by selecting the best people possible, providing them the best possible training in behavioral techniques to develop and control groups, and of insuring that they are given the fullest logistical support in carrying out their work, cannot be overemphasized. These people, as far as the client is concerned, are the program, and only the best will do.[12]

In addition, the management techniques outlined in Chapter 2 (as well as in Chapter 6) must be provided to extension staff.

THE ROLE OF INTERNATIONAL BUSINESS AS AN EXTERNAL INITIATOR OF CHANGE

In talking about organizational change and training, a heavy reliance so far in this book has been on public, government-sponsored agencies that have specific responsibilities for target groups within a country. Yet another external group to be considered is the international company.

It has been convenient to genuflect upon the conventional wisdom from the 1960s that the role of international companies in Third World countries is primarily that of exploitation of both cheap labor and resources. Certainly there has been enough of that throughout the history of the industrial revolution. Today's modern effort of exploitation, called production sharing, is only the newest chapter of a sorry history. In this process, components for finished products are produced in a myriad of countries (all at the lowest cost possible) and then assembled into a final unit at a country that provides even cheaper labor.

Yet one should not turn one's back upon the possibility (under the right circumstances) of using multinationals as agents for instituting external change. One must recognize that despite their ethical failings, their undimensional quest to make a buck, they are also highly efficient instruments—which, if properly coopted, can benefit developing countries. That desire for profit can be integrated into development efforts and serve as a model for change whereby the company gets its buck and the host country gets an external change agent. But the circumstances surrounding the interaction of the multinational must be carefully controlled. Two examples are provided in this section.

The first is an integrated area development project in the Philippines in the island-province of Leyte. In this example, multinational companies (instead of governmental agencies) served as the prime innovators. The basic philosophy behind the company's operations in this experiment was totally alien from conventional multinationals. Company officials supposedly felt that "the total system approach (integrated development) attempts to identify areas of mutual interest between indigenous citizen groups and potential investors prior to the initiation of a project." This is in contrast to a traditional multinational linear approach, "where a multi-national enterprise enters a region exclusively in search of market opportunities in its major area of business activity, with limited concern for the socio-economic environment."[13]

In this organizational change strategy, instead of trying to change existing organizations and the people they serve, a new organizational structure using multinationals (which will receive a reasonable profit during the time they are involved) served as the core for effecting change and development in the area. Such an integrated program goes through stages, as defined in this project:

1. Prime contractor. A firm is selected to manage the overall project, providing the necessary financial and managerial resources to manage the project from start to finish. Up-front costs are primarily absorbed by the prime contractors. In addition, a special understanding and training of the managers in that company is made. For example, chief executive officers are counseled to cultivate a genuine interest in understanding the social, political, and economic objectives of the host countries they serve.

2. Systematic staging of operations (agriculture).

    a. Subsistence phase. In the case of agriculture, this phase focuses on developing the infrastructure needed to increase productivity.

    b. Income-earning phase. Income of farmers within the project area theoretically will be raised by the increase in productivity, and the excess capital then can be used for additional projects such as livestock raising and cottage industries.

    c. Investors' phrase. Surplus earnings, as the income base rises, are set aside as savings. Farmers become part owners in projects such as animal feed, milk, and processing and manage their own credit unions.

d. Mangers' phase. The external international agencies are phased out, farmers take control of all the developed infrastructure, but host government agencies continue to serve target members with guidance and advice.[14]

In this example, the development of the sub-A basin in Leyte, the principal companies involved were the National Grains Authority and a private company, Bancom Farm Services Corporation. As of the sources' publication in 1981, the project was only in its initial stage of draining swamplands. One wonders, given the corrupt practices of the Marcos regime, whether joint development, despite how good it sounds, ever took place.

One tends to be somewhat skeptical about any real effort to satisfy basic human needs in the Philippines during the Marcos regime, and in fact more recent news from that country, in part due to the collapse of sugar prices, indicates that farmers were being kicked off of their landholdings, prior to the Aquino takeover.

Yet this development plan, which is almost too simplistic (since it basically is a rewrite of the Rostow stages of development within a country, which has been rather well documented as a failure), could serve as a vehicle for external-sponsored change within a country.

Certainly, if corporations come in with relatively benign objectives to help themselves at a modest, reasonable level (yet focused on directly helping the people within the area they affect), the way by which they run their operations could certainly serve as an organizational model for other agencies within the country. This is not an especially new proposal. One reason why it has not been effective is that corporations have not chosen to facilitate and nurture that spin-off process to the host country. Corporations, for example, are good at eliminating bureaucratic overhead in the routine management of their operations. Their training of workers leans more toward promoting efficiency in job functions. It would be interesting to see the result if a lean and mean corporate-directed company were allowed into a specific country and given a region to develop (with the specific objective of satisfying the basic human needs of the people within that region—in addition to making a profit). If, for example, the company were placed in competition with a government-run development agency in a similar region, with the overall objective of showing which organization does the best job (identifying specifically what differentiates one organization from the other), such an experiment could be especially illuminating.

Initiating change strategies by external means, however, is more commonly associated with international efforts to provide training to specific individuals within specific organizations in specific countries. It has long been a dream that multinationals could play a major role in that process. They will need farsighted leaders who understand the role of participation in development. Unfortunately, based on what is happening in U.S. business schools in the area of international business (where the emphasis has been in viewing the Third World as a market rather than a development target for change), the chances of developing those people are not all that promising.

In a sense, business schools themselves would need an external stimulus to initiate a change strategy to reform their educational processes—that is, if one believes that educating young, potential business people in the value of a world community and a fair deal for host countries is possible in the first place.

At the current moment, the education of such people is largely restricted to how one can distort the cultural and political realities of a given foreign environment to maximize making a buck without being nationalized or kidnapped in the process. This is a very narrow, shortsighted perspective that will continue to cause the United States difficulties in trying to compete in a world market in the twenty-first century. Perhaps the guiding philosophy is best summed up by an interview with a business dean who lamented on "the difficulty of teaching young students how to bribe effectively." Schools in the United States are certainly not alone in this feeling. Currently there is an enormous drive by U.S. students to get business degrees and make a living (in too many U.S. campuses the enrollment in business schools approaches half the total enrollment), and most are given the ethics training of a slime mold. This is not a comforting thought due to the effect these people will have in building a world community in the early twenty-first century. Consequently, the Heenan/Perlmutter model outlined in the Philippine example of how international companies might play a positive role as external change initiators is mostly wishful thinking at the moment. There are, however, some outstanding examples of corporate behavior, and an example from Colombia will be provided as the last example of this chapter.

A Positive Corporate Case Example of Effecting Change

The final example is of a cooperative banana company operating in Colombia. The zone of operation is in a particularly backward part of the country where little infrastructure exists. Consequently, there was a desire to expand the base of operations beyond that of bananas in order to pay the costs of developing the company's own infrastructure. A young engineer, who had worked with the English-based, Intermediate Technology Development Center, was hired as project manager to manage the development effort. His skill and dedication brought amazing results. First an extension staff was trained in group development techniques, and permission was granted from top management to allow farmers to become involved in the design and decision-making aspects of the development program. With that input, it was discovered that waste bananas were a major problem for disposal and that farmers were interested in agricultural production other than just bananas. The project manager, specially trained in appropriate technology, and his extension staff ultimately created a series of nested technologies (supported by the cooperative members since they worked in the design phases of the project) that greatly expanded the variety of agricultural production and the standard of living in the area.[15]

Waste bananas were fed to cattle penned in permanent sheds. The manure from the animals falls onto a declined floor, and the mass moves by gravity to a biogas digester. In that gravitational flow, ducks are allowed to forage, thoroughly mixing the animal wastes in the flow to the digester. The digester makes both methane gas (which is used for cooking and lighting in the farmhouse) and a nitrogen-enriched liquid fertilizer. Part of the fertilizer is used in fish ponds to fertilize pond growth for an additional agriculture program, and the rest is used to fertilize truck gardens, banana trees, corn, and range grass. The nonedible biomass and range grass from the fertilized fields are, in turn, fed to the cattle, making a closed, pollution-free, agricultural system producing bananas, vegetables, corn, beef, poultry, fish, and fuel.

The importance of this example is the involvement of the beneficiaries with the management and extension staff of the company, who had been both hired and trained with the specific intention that the beneficiaries have something important to contribute to the development of programs that affect them. Furthermore, it is also equally important that the company waited, in carrying out the project, until as many training variables as possible were controlled. Consequently, as an example the extension staff was adequately trained to understand and utilize the power of organized beneficiaries in carrying out the project, in direct contrast to the Central American example presented earlier in the chapter. That such a successful effort was carried out by an international company (which like all companies is motivated to make a respectable buck) shows that even such a conventionally disparaged external change source is capable of improving the lives of Third World citizens, under properly designed circumstances.

Analysis of the Program Managers

The project manager of the Colombian banana company fit solidly in the humanistic, operant conditioning mode of behavior. He knew instinctively the right time to compliment an employee, which he did with genuine sincerity for he knew his mission was righteous (so to speak). His skills helped both the company and the people of the region. Unquestionably, the skills of the manager were the pivotal factors for the organizational changes introduced in the project. Such a key person is invaluable for initiating change (the successful Central American example also had an effective, humanistic, key person serving as project manager).

The point is that just about anybody who really cares can become effective in the use of behavioral technologies such as operant conditioning. In *Walden II*, one of the central characters says, "positive reinforcement is just another way of saying love."[16] Most project managers do not like to use that word since, too often, they are expected to have a cynical view of people that borders more on hate. But to a large extent, love is really what we are talking about, or at least a workable concern for each other as Gwynne Dyer has described it earlier in the chapter. If the managers of a change program do not have a basic love or concern for the people they serve, there is precious little that can be done through training to improve their effectiveness.

The manager of the fruit-processing plant operated in a similar manner. While she was not formally educated as the Colombian manager was, she had an intuitive grasp of how to use positive reinforcement techniques and involve the entire community in planning, designing, and developing the project. Third World change agencies need to base their change efforts on these kind of people. The problem is to recruit and train them.

The final point to be made is that in-country change institutions can routinely recruit and train such people, and this should become a primary strategy for internal change efforts. Chapter 5 will provide an explanation of how such institutions can be developed, and what kinds of training we might find in them, to produce humanistic personnel.

SUMMARY

The initiation of change efforts is a complex process involving a multitude of variables that can positively or negatively affect the process. Unfortunately, many of those variables are difficult to control and, in some cases, may be uncontrollable.

There are two primary methods to go about initiating change. The first is through external sources such as international development agencies whose primary mission is to help Third World countries. Earlier in the chapter, it was shown that geopolitics enters this process, and both the Eastern bloc and Western bloc countries are active in trying to help the Third World—each in its own unique style.

The other primary method of change is through internal sources. Such sources have the advantage of greater control by the host-country government, but often have the disadvantage of not being able to recruit suitably trained indigenous people to implement the training required in making organizational changes. In such cases, one can coopt the external approach by hiring short-term expatriates to handle some of the training.

The ultimate question, in initiating and carrying out organizational change, is the kind of personnel training an organization should utilize. The pragmatic suggestion is that the training should focus on teaching people how they can work together effectively—without necessarily establishing a specific or deep affection for each other.

The long-term objective of this training, then, is to produce personnel who will be effective in using behavioral technologies and who accept participation as a philosophical and operational base in their efforts to improve organizations. With that objective in mind, a specific behavioral technology, operant conditioning, was described; a strong suggestion made was that, because change always involves conflict, a better way to facilitate the change process is to use the positive reinforcement component of operant conditioning. Such a technology complements and facilitates the difficult task of carrying out organizational change.

Most definitely, it is believed that an autocratic approach is inappropriate, and the nature and limitations of using autocratic approaches have been presented, with fairly consistent literature to support this position. If one is serious about making organizational changes and creating designs for the twenty-first century, then nineteenth century autocratic processes have no positive role.

The final sections dealt with some specific case examples of change efforts in the Third World. There are examples of both good and bad ways to go about initiating changes. The primary point to be made by the example was to back up the central message of Chapter 2, namely, that participation, operant conditioning, involvement of the host community, and group decision making all increase the probability of designing and initiating successful change efforts. A reliance on autocracy, indifference, and centralized nonbeneficiary-involved change efforts more often promotes a long-term failure.

Finally, the role of international corporations, with two case examples of corporate behavior, were presented. One example in Colombia was highly successful. It is not known whether the Philippine example was successful or even initiated. Based on political realities during the past two decades, one has a reason to be skeptical.

While the focus of this book is upon host-country national change agencies and international change agencies that interface with Third World countries, there should be more concern about involvement of international corporations (but little more can be spent on them in this book). The fact is that they could play an important role in Third World development if harnessed properly and regulated through some kind of international controlling agent. Obviously, the United Nations with its current inability to do much of anything is not a viable choice. Perhaps an international stockholder's cartel of concerned stockholders might do the job. The current effort on U.S. campuses to get corporations out of South Africa is a case in point. As a process that could be expanded with the right kind of organization and leaders, such a cartel could certainly be more effective than another United Nations resolution.

Unfortunately, the best that can be said for multinationals is that they are not at present an effective force for initiating change. Unfortunately, and especially so for U.S. corporations, the current practice of exporting the United States' most dirty and tedious jobs to the world's poor at Dickensian wages is not only hurting the poor in this country, who used to do those jobs and no longer can, but is creating an image of the United States being the great Satan of international worker exploitation. It is an image that tarnishes what the country stands for and, more importantly, does not facilitate the initiation of international organization change efforts. Regretfully, at present the United States does not set an example of what the designs for the twenty-first century should be.

NOTES

1. Allen Jedlicka, from field notes during a summer study in 1982.

2. Allen Jedlicka, from field notes on Zuni reservation industrialization analysis, summer 1968.

3. Morris Solomon and Flemming Heegard, "An Action-Training Strategy for Project Management," Development Project Management Center, International Training, ERS/FDD, U.S. Department of Agriculture, Washington, D.C., 1977, mimeographed.

4. K. Lewin, R. Lippitt, and R. K. White, "Patterns of Aggressive Behavior in Experimentally Created Social Climates," *Journal of Social Psychology* 10 (1939).

5. Gwynne Dyer, *WAR* (New York: Crown, 1985), p. 264.

6. Allen Jedlicka and Tim Eibes, "Behavioral Energy Management," proceedings of the Seventh Annual Industrial Energy Technology Conference, May, 1985, Houston, Texas.

7. "Where Skinner's Theories Work," *Business Week,* December 2, 1972, p. 64.

8. Ibid.

9. Allen Jedlicka, *Organization for Rural Development* (New York: Praeger, 1977), p. 38.

10. Douglas McGregor, "The Human Side of Enterprise," in *Some Theories of Organization,* ed. Albert Publication and Chadwick Halverstroh (Homewood, Ill.: Irwin-Dorsey, 1960), p. 180.

11. Allen Jedlicka, from field notes during summer study in Central America, 1977.

12. Jedlicka, *Organization for Rural Development, p.* 38.

13. David Heenan and Howard Perlmutter, *Multinational Organization Development: A Social Architectural Perspective* (Manila: Addison-Wesley, 1981), p. 56.

14. Ibid., p. 128.

15. Allen Jedlicka, "Resource Free Energy Generation Systems," *Interciencia* 4 (May-June 1979), p. 45.

16. B. F. Skinner, *Walden II* (New York: Free Press, 1948).

5

The Development of Third World Organizational Change Institutions and Training Mechanisms

In the decadent western countries, man exploits man. But in the socialist paradise we have risen above all this. Our behavior is just the opposite.

Anonymous Pole

INTRODUCTION

In the Third World, viewed from a socialist standpoint, man does indeed exploit man. The ultimate objective of organizational change, and a democratic involvement of the people who are affected by change efforts, is to insure that in the name of progress the Polish reality is not created.

In earlier chapters it has been argued that a major reason for many of the problems that exist in Third World countries is that the organizations charged with positively affecting a particular group of beneficiaries do not have the managerial skills or philosophy to involve those beneficiaries in the development of effective programs. Chapter 2 presented some "classical" ways by which management can improve that design process and involvement of beneficiaries. It has also been strongly argued that one way to accomplish that is through the development of multicultural analysis teams, consisting of members of the cultures of both the change organization and the beneficiaries. Structurally, there is a strong relationship between the teams and change efforts. It is through multicultural teams that an organization will be able to get the environmental and cultural information that makes effective solutions possible—solutions, because they have been a part of the development that beneficiaries will support.

The obvious difficulty with such a structural arrangement is that the autocratic orientation of the management of too many Third World change organizations has a rather pejorative view of beneficiary abilities and tends to resist efforts to change its style of performance. In many cases such people will have to

be either removed or rehabilitated. Given the limited success in reforming ha-
bitual autocrats, as discussed in Chapter 3, the greater likelihood will be removal of such people to positions where they will not be dangerous. However,
given the pattern of nepotism and outright corruption that too often has put such
people in positions of authority in the first place, it will be difficult to remove
them without a national policy and political commitment to do so. Currently,
the Aquino government in the Philippines is beginning just such a process by
removing Marcos officials throughout government agencies. At this writing,
we are hearing vague rumblings of warlord depredations in the rural areas, that
deposed Marcos appointees are creating their own regional governments and
causing a great deal of conflict as the process is carried out. But if the Aquino
reformation effort is successful, it could stand out as a classic example of what
must be done in creating an effective organizational change and involving beneficiaries in the process of that change.

The current efforts in the Philippines will have to be repeated throughout the
Third World, and the Aquino government will do the world a favor by carefully
documenting how they carry out that process.

COMMITMENT BY TOP MANAGEMENT

One of the paramount concerns in building or developing a change institution is the need for commitment and support by the top levels of management.
If the top management does not support changing the organization so that there
is stronger emphasis on involving beneficiaries in the development process,
then individuals would indeed be foolish to initiate such efforts on their own
without line authority since they more likely would find themselves out of a job.

The commitment and support of top management, to a large extent, must
become a national policy. However, there are rare instances where particularly
charismatic individuals can effect such changes on their own. The long-term
reality is that commitment to effect change must be provided by national leaders,
as has been done most recently in China. With this introduction in mind,
acknowledging the political realities in the process of organizational change
(namely, that ultimately politics will dictate the nature of organizational change),
the remainder of the chapter will discuss the issue of developing in-country
change institutions and processes.

IN-COUNTRY ORGANIZATIONAL CHANGE INSTITUTIONS AND PROCESSES

Much of this book has described various techniques that can be used to
change organizations and, of course, has emphasized the need for participation
by beneficiaries. It has stressed that a top-downward process, by consultant

experts or management, does not have a complete reality base for decision making; thus, improper decisions will be made and program efforts may not serve the people.

A traditional way of trying to minimize that effect is by the organizational development of in-country change institutions that will handle the training of people who then theoretically will carry out organizational change in a manner more beneficial to the people the organization serves.

It is important to realize that, just because such a process is in-country and not dominated by expatriate experts, this does not automatically mean it will be successful. Involvement of expatriates will probably continue to be a fact of life for some time since most countries do not have sufficient indigenous training resources. An example of an improperly designed indigenous change effort was offered in Chapter 3. The Tanzanian program relied on nonreality-based assumptions regarding how different regional cultures would react to change efforts in the Ujamaa system. Hence, it serves as a prime example of nonclient-centered thinking. Had the originators of the system involved members of all client cultural groups in the initial planning (as presented in Chapter 2 on group decision making), there certainly is a chance that the desired changes could have been developed in such ways as to be acceptable to all the potential beneficiaries (or scrapped if it had been shown that there was no way to accommodate the objectives of the change organization's leaders and the realities of the regional cultures it serves). A similar process was observed by the writer among Bolivian extension agents where the project planning was so indifferent and careless that young men from former haciendado families (landholders prior to the land tenure revolution of 1952, which held fellow villagers as serfs) were selected to be extension agents. No amount of training of interpersonal communication skills for these young men could have improved their effectiveness. Because of the political history of the community (and the fact that the liberated former "serfs" viewed them as pariahs), they were doomed to be ineffective from the beginning. Consequently, it is essential to understand that within any country there are cultural differences and that those differences must be accounted for if the training of the people who implement organizational changes is to be effective. Those cultural differences must be included in the development of change organizations.

To that end cultural anthropology plays an essential part in the change institution for it enables managers to examine the basic assumptions of both their culture and the cultures of the people they serve. While that may seem tautological, in actuality, too much of Third World change efforts is still dominated by the professional view that change does not have to consider culture. It is maintained that people will do as you say regardless of the effect of their culture.

One way to establish cultural accommodation, in the process of changing an organization, is through the inclusion of an organizational or team anthropologist who can factor in the effects of client culture into the training of organizational members. Another way is actually to use members of specific cultural groups in the retraining process of organizational staff.

The U.S. Peace Corps, during one of its phases of training, has used just such an approach of bringing in representatives of local cultures that the potential Peace Corps volunteer would live with. In this way, the trainees are provided with a firsthand account of cultural differences. (One must recognize that the Peace Corps is a bureaucratic organization whose purse strings are subject to the whims of congressional tightening—in good years a good job is done; in bad years a not-so-good job is done.)

Another mode of examining the basic cultural assumptions within a given country is by performing an individual and group audit of how they perceive different cultures. The intent is to follow some of the Lewin approach on unfreezing and refreezing attitudes toward different cultures. Organization members formulate what the differences are (unfreezing) and try to replace irrational assumptions with a more rational understanding of differences with the help of a trained facilitator (refreezing). The specific means by which this can be done will be described in detail in Chapter 6. But one final note will be made. When one initiates such training in an indigenous organization, it must be across the board instead of with isolated groups within the organization. Without a complete commitment to understanding cultural differences by all members of the organization, changes among only a few will probably result in a great deal of frustration by those few, for they will stand alone, changed in their attitudes, within an organization that remains unchanged.

THE NEED FOR MODIFYING WESTERN TRAINING TECHNIQUES

Many of the techniques that have been proposed in Chapter 2 have an obvious Western bias. As expatriates we assume that non-Westerners will interact effectively with training procedures that work well with us. However, modifications are often necessary although the degree to which those techniques have to be modified will vary with the culture. As an example, the writer's training experience has been primarily with Nahualt speakers in Mexico, the Quechua peoples of Bolivia, and Mestizo groups in Honduras and El Salvador—among people who were not exactly well educated by our standards. The main variable to control in the use of Western techniques was the assumption that participants already had a previous knowledge of what you were describing. Thus, it was important to spend more time in explaining the objective of the exercise and checking to make sure that people really understood what you were saying. For the most part, participants behaved in a more responsible manner than do undergraduates doing similar kinds of training exercises and were capable of doing very complex training exercises such as the interpretive structural modeling technique described in Chapter 2.

Some obvious changes are commonly necessary. For example, if the exercises involve setting a descriptive scene under which the training takes place and an unmodified Western exercise depicts a scene of commuting on a New York subway train, one would have to change the setting to something consistent with the cultural background of the trainees.

It is this area where teamwork between outside sources, local professionals, and beneficiaries plays an important role. It smooths out some of the cultural quirks that can limit the effectiveness of a training tool and facilitates modifications that will make the training exercises useful.

CREATING AN INDIGENOUS STAFF BY EXPATRIATE TRAINING

A time-honored tradition of establishing an in-house cadre of training staff is to train them outside the organization and return them to their home organizations. There are, however, some problems with that strategy, as Solomon and Heegard describe:

It creates an artificial environment in which individuals are temporarily taken out of their organization to be taught concepts and techniques. Upon returning from training, each individual is surrounded by colleagues and superiors whose experience, knowledge, and customary ways of working are different from what the trainee has learned. It is the rare individual who can apply what was learned in training within his organization, even when the training was appropriate and effective.[1]

What that warning really states is that piecemeal training, which unfortunately is what most international agencies offer to Third World countries, is ineffective. A better long-term strategy for developing an effective in-country change institution is to utilize a strategy of building an in-house training capability, which will be used for long-term change of the organization.

BUILDING IN-HOUSE TRAINING CAPABILITY

One of the international agencies most involved in training overseas managers for organizational change efforts has been USDA's Development Project Management Center based in Washington.[2]

The approach of this organization is to rely upon an in-country training and consulting team. From the perspective of the organization, a team could utilize three or four full-time host-national staff members. The assortment of skills of these people would include financial manager/economist, management specialists, engineers, organization development and training specialists, and specific specialists depending upon the exact mission of the organization (agronomists for agricultural programs, medical doctors for birth control programs, and so on). The emphasis is upon a multidisciplinary understanding and philosophical background of all members of the team. Also included is the ability to relate with others, "in a collaborative rather than a professional or bureaucratic mode."[3] It is suggested that the indigenous team will initially require some help from outside consultants, and suggestions on how that may be accomplished were presented in Chapter 4.

Finally, it is recommended that the team "spend some time in 'team building' activities which focus on how a group can function more effectively, establishing the goals of the group . . . and how they can function more effectively in their environment."[4] The center rightly suggests that "team building activities are best carried out in an atmosphere where people feel free to practice new patterns of relationships in a non-threatening atmosphere."[5] However, beyond such simplistic but never the less valid statements, the remaining suggestions for team building are greatly lacking for several reasons. First, the "team is seen as a service arm of the organization that has overall responsibility for the project." There is no expressed involvement of beneficiaries in team building. Second, the team is provided instruction and direction by top management, which includes "objectives, budget constraints, coverage, and general constraints." These instructions should be regarded as provisional and are subject to renegotiation by the working groups. Finally, the strategy "presupposes that top management is willing to share on a de-facto basis their influence on the shaping of projects with their subordinates, even though they reserve the final decisions to themselves."[6]

Unfortunately, this kind of structure will not suffice for it still leaves primary decision making in the hands of the top management officials who apparently listen, somewhat, to team members but nevertheless make the final decisions by themselves. It is not unlike the typical head of department-faculty committee process in a U.S. university where the administrator appoints a committee to carry out a study, which is allowed to relay their fact finding to him. Whereupon he, more often, promptly carries out his own predetermined decision and proclaims he has been participative in his administrative practices. In other words, the approach, as described, sounds more like the typical U.S. administrative practice of creating quasi-democratic institutions while still concentrating (but not sharing) the power by the top or central administrations.

In light of what has already been written in this book, such a strategy ignores the pivotal role of "the milieu [which] contains many organizational, political, social and cultural forces which may be helpful or dysfunctional from the point of view of development. These forces have to be dealt with in ways which facilitate the desired development outcomes while respecting the legitimate interests of the groups involved."[7] That is exactly the point. Those groups must be involved if one is to build an effective in-house training capability. A top-downward managerial approach more likely will not include those forces.

In establishing training objectives, top management must be willing to allow the presence of beneficiaries and accept that these people have some idea of what is needed to effect change in their lives. Their input must become an integral part of the training of staff through in-house training.

REGIONAL EXAMPLES OF THE IMPORTANCE OF INVOLVING BENEFICIARIES IN PLANNING CHANGE

Two examples are offered to show the importance of involving clients in that objective formulation process. One case is from West Africa and the other from Puebla, Mexico.

Developmental approaches in the rural area of the state of Puebla, prior to the introduction of the Puebla Project, followed the traditional expert-service organizational philosophy that is so consistently used throughout the world. It is a philosophy that maximizes top-downward decision making.

Experts from service organizations in an ill-planned, desultory manner would contact villagers (more often on an individual basis) and attempt to supply information and input to farmers in the region. This was typically done in an autocratic style that made even more poignant the fact that they often did not know what they were talking about. In fairness to what existed before, selection and training of extension agents were usually inadequate, case loads were too high, and logistical support was lacking. Consequently, farmers viewed national services as a joke and, furthermore, became suspicious that the real motive behind interaction with agency officials was some kind of political control. As indicated in the quote on the first page of Chapter 1, the farmers resented the lack of their involvement in the change process.

With that recognized background, representatives of the Puebla Project, trained in the manner described in Chapter 3, initiated a joint objective determination process with farmers throughout the area. One objective was to introduce hybrid corn to the area. Farmers did not like that alternative because they did not like the taste of hybrid corn or the expense of buying seed.[8] Upon further negotiation, seed trials were established, and it was found that native varieties would produce about as well, and in some cases better, than hybrid seed with the proper amount of fertilizer. So clearly in this case, decision making was not left solely in the hands of top management since the interaction between managers and beneficiaries resulted in the recognition and finally adoption of a better alternative than the original choice of the organization. Viewing the process as an operant-conditioning exercise, the project administration created a situation the beneficiaries liked (use of native seed varieties with improved fertilizer application) by removing a situation they did not want (expensive hybrid seed with synthetic fertilizer). Such a simple yet effective solution required only one really difficult modification, the training of an agency's staff to accept

the fact that solutions to problems must include the interaction of those for whom the solutions will be developed.

An example with the opposite result is the development of an irrigated rice irrigation project in Guinea-Bissau. This country is characterized by autocratic, centralized planning along the Soviet model of agriculture—a tested model that has had a notable lack of success but was adopted because the Soviet Union helped Guinea in the war for independence from Portugal.

Someone in the central administration decided, after receiving a gift of irrigation pumps from a European country, that the pumps could be used to grow paddy rice, in an effort to increase rice production and supply during the dry months. The intention was good, but the project was carried out without any involvement of the people it was intended to help. Land near rivers was conscripted from the farmers who owned it, and bulldozers more or less leveled the area and built a crude outer containment perimeter around the field. Water was then continually pumped into the paddy on basically a 24-hour-basis from the beginning of the project until the end. Because of the lack of participation by local farmers, the government found out, ultimately, that the soil was too sandy to hold water. Consequently, it was necessary to pump water continuously. Because the ground was not uniformly leveled, weed growth was a major problem and without herbicides grew almost unchecked. Additionally, black water fever from the river water was an ever-present danger for the field workers. The end product was a small amount of very poor quality rice that cost considerably more than imported rice to grow.[9]

In this case, the farmers whose lands had been conscripted knew perfectly well that it was not suitable for paddy—but no one asked them. Under the circumstances, even if they had been asked what motive would they have for telling agriculture officials about the major drawbacks to using the land, since the land had been conscripted from them.

Obviously, failure to involve the farmer in the decision-making process resulted in the failure of a major governmental initiative, for in the end the land could not be effectively used for paddy and was not available for sorghum production—its original use. Because of the negative reinforcement (conscription of the land), a great deal of mistrust of the government was rightly generated, among all farmers in the region. Commitment to a long outdated ideology (the use of centralized planning without feedback from the people the planning serves) insured the failure of the project regardless of how benign the original objectives might have been. The lack of willingness of top management to develop an organization that would involve beneficiaries in the design of the project assured the failure of the program. This is particularly noteworthy since, as a consequence of the revolution, administrators had the chance to build organizations from the ground up.

Even the Puebla Project had some difficulty in obtaining total involvement. For example, one regional zone did not desire to use synthetic fertilizer, a cornerstone of the project. Neither management nor the villagers could agree on the issue, and in the end that zone did not enter the program. Three years later, in an ironic twist, that zone's fears of becoming dependent on buying synthetic fertilizer (the farmers used compost and manure) were vindicated when the petroleum crisis skyrocketed the price of the very limited supply of synthetic fertilizer. In a scramble to help other farmers in the program, extension agents tried rapidly to diffuse composting techniques. In the short run, crops failed in the zones that had become dependent on synthetic fertilizer.

One could argue, from hindsight, that the viewpoints of farmers in the zone that avoided synthetic fertilizer should have been considered and acted upon. A contingency program of organic techniques should have been created from the start. So in the end even an excellent program such as Puebla suffered because of a partial nonparticipatory involvement more characteristic of the program in Guinea-Bissau.

POWER AND CONTROL IN CHANGE ORGANIZATIONS

As has been stated several times, a crucial issue in changing organizations is the element of power and control. The issue is no less important to developing effective in-country institutions. Much of what has been expressed in earlier chapters is the idea of reforming the existing, centralized, bureaucratized professional service organizations. Certainly that is what USDA, the OAS, and the World Bank do, and they have spent many years trying to carry out the reformation process through expatriate training programs—for the most part with limited success. That is not completely the fault of the training programs, for a common phenomenon is that, after people complete a training program in some area such as project management, they become a valuable commodity for higher-paying jobs in the private sector and move on. The most ineffective tend to stay behind, particularly in countries that provide reasonable retirement funds. Power remains centralized within the change organization's bureaucracy.

Bruce Stakes presents an alternative approach where organizational change efforts would be designed to set up community development programs that largely function under local or individual control.[10] The emphasis is that such efforts should *not* be controlled or supplied by the existing centralized government service agencies. While such agencies could provide some limited technical and subsidy support, the intention would be to minimize the dependency typically created in a bureaucracy-dominated format. The question is how to create change institutions that will have the power and authority to train the people who can carry out such a radical organizational change. That ultimately comes to a policy decision that is determined by someone in a political position.

Political decision undeniably is the most uncontrollable variable in the whole organizational change process. More often it will not be made because of vested interests, or if it is made, it will be implemented in such a way as to create even more chaos even if the original intention was to redress bureaucratic excesses in the process of development. The Ujamaa example in Tanzania discussed in Chapter 3 is a classic example of how trying to reform the bureaucracy produces a worse alternative.

Consequently, if we are to talk about developing organizational change institutions that will provide the kind of innovative leadership that will lead to greater community involvement and control, we are ultimately talking about bureaucratic reformation. Korten, among others, has emphasized reorienting bureaucratic organizations by training bureaucrats to have a greater social and community understanding.[11] The ultimate focus would be on how to strengthen community-level action and involvement into the bureaucratic organization so that, for example, Stakes's original concern of minimizing the dependency of beneficiaries on a central change organization can be achieved while still supplying essential technical and infrastructure elements.[12]

If top management is resolved to make the kind of organizational changes needed for greater community involvement, and the political power is committed for the change, people can be trained to carry out the process.

As examples of situations where power has directed policy decisions (for better or worse) in community involvement, the macro-change efforts of China and India will be profiled in the following section.

EXAMPLES OF MACRO-SIZED EFFORTS OF CLIENT IN-VOLVEMENT IN THE CHANGE PROCESS

If we were to look at Third World internally motivated and managed organizational changes on a macro-scale, we would find two countries that serve as highly visible experiments on community involvement:

1. India is being suffocated by an overbearing bureaucracy, and the organizational change experiment has not yet begun and probably never will.
2. In China the experiment is well underway and may even lead to an increase of democracy producing its own version of democratic socialism.

India, which is a worst-case scenario, will be examined first. If ever there was need for organizational change and a need for bureaucratic reform, India is one country that needs both.

Looking at the bureaucracy first, the country is literally suffocated in paperwork, requiring several copies of bureaucrat-signed documents for management activities that would require no documentation or paperwork in other countries. Because of the political patronage system, there is a strong resistance to initiating changes that could streamline the process. After all, if someone is laid off, that probably antagonizes the relative or friend who hired the person in the first place and may lead to reprisals upon other relatives of the worker who made the decision to eliminate some excess labor.

There have, however, been efforts to introduce a certain element of participation into the design of development programs through an innovative, decentralized, television project. A pilot system linked with India's INSAT satellite systems (serving 5 million people) called KATA sends organizational representatives to villages and measures reactions to the system's educational programming. Direct feedback is obtained from small groups in a cross-section of villages in order to develop new programs that address the specific questions and input received from the small-group decision process.

In a unique innovation in the project, villagers even play the role of actors in programs addressing specific messages such as hygiene and birth control. The training of organization administrators to accept the involvement of viewers has played an important role in this project. Of course, a consistent point of this book is that change organization members need to be trained to accept the involvement of beneficiaries. While the program has been successful, the problem is one of scale. Affecting 5 million people in a country of 800 million really only amounts to being a pilot project.

A crucial social issue addressed by KATA is the caste system. Many of the programs are addressed to the untouchable caste. Despite its official termination, caste is an issue that will always make participative approaches difficult in the country for lower-caste people do not participate with higher-caste people. Existing for thousands of years, one can predict that the caste system will not change before the twenty-first century. The statistics surrounding development in the country are truly staggering. Over 400 million out of 800 million Indians are officially designated as living in poverty (and that is Indian poverty). In order to provide an education to all the country's children, a schoolhouse would have to be built every five minutes. Seventy percent of the water supply is polluted, 80 percent of all villages have no electricity, nine out of ten villagers own no land—the list goes on and on with the final statistic being that the country will have over a billion people by the year 2000. Indira Ghandi reportedly said, shortly before her assassination, that the backwardness of the country allows it to eclipse the industrial revolution in the development of twenty-first century technologies and industry because India never had a chance to participate in the original industrial revolution. India will have to recognize that, in that quest, it competes with Japan, the United States, Europe, and even South Korea—all countries that have substantially smaller populations and better infrastructure.

Undoubtedly, the country's massive population and long tradition of inequality will continue to hinder all development efforts. Despite the fact that the Indian system is a democracy, the effects of caste and position negate much that democracy stands for, and in the sense of social equality, the Chinese system embodies a view that is more similar to the U.S. concept of democracy than India will probably ever have. The prognosis for organizational designs of the future is that India's experiment in organizational change has not really begun and will do so only with great difficulty.

China as a behavioral example was presented in Chapter 2, where the use of groups and group pressure upon citizens has led to successes in rapid change, but at the expense of what many Westerners would call personal freedom. Of particular effectiveness has been the use of small groups in birth control programs to convince deviant members that they should follow the party line. Of course, the example provided in Chapter 2 focused on how expectant parents are pressured to accept abortion through various positive reinforcement (operant conditioning) techniques. For example, formal recognition is given in the factory where the mother works that she has been a good citizen by accepting abortion, and guarantees are made that her single child will be provided a university education (along with threats that some of the government privileges for the family will be revoked if she does not agree). Unfortunately (in some cases), in the end a forced abortion of the fetus sometimes as late as the seventh month is imposed upon deviant mothers. Such a reality gives a bad press to operant conditioning, but one must also question whether the very real possibility of that fetus starving to death somewhere about 2010 after 24 years of chronic malnutrition is a better alternative before the Chinese strategy is condemned out of hand. This is, after all, what currently happens to too large a percentage of the Indian population—and could happen to the Chinese population.

OPERANT CONDITIONING PRACTICES IN CHINA

In terms of using operant conditioning, China is more advanced compared to the United States. As an example, in my secondary role as an energy conservation consultant, I have promoted the use of verbal reinforcers by energy managers to get employees to do simple things (on a consistent basis) such as shutting off lights and machinery when they are not being used. Praise for performing a desired behavior is a simple reinforcer. The discussions during the workshop training inevitably focus on the violation of human rights, the constraints to freedom, and even "communist brainwashing." All of this is advanced for proposing a very simple act, mainly that supervisors compliment their subordinates when they perform a positive act such as turning off the lights. This is something they should be doing anyway, and the reluctance and dismay that are so often expressed probably have more to do with the deep-seated administrative cultural view in the United States that we are unique individuals not subject to behavioral control. Operant conditioning is really no more than the golden rule, "do unto others as you would have them do unto you," instead of the prevalent U.S. management creed of "do unto others before they do you in."

Industrial practices in China and, in some cases Japan, provide useful examples. Administrators actually come out into the workplace and talk with workers, inquiring about how things are going not only with their job, but with their family. Administrators compliment workers for doing a good job and even post announcements about superior work done by particularly outstanding employees. That may all sound pretentious, but it is effective.

The Chinese have set up a powerful behavioral experiment that, in combination with the relaxing of government controls, may unleash an economic expansion that will make us gasp in comparison to our present complaints about the economic competition of Japan. The elements are all there. If the political and bureaucratic reformation can be continued to support democratic organizational changes, the basic, underlying participative nature of Chinese society, industry, and interpersonal relations can lead to a massive Rostowian takeoff into sustained economic growth.

The point to be made, in reference to China, is that the Chinese have pretty much followed the imperatives of using behavioral technology and participation that are prerequisites for the development of Third World change organizations. Going through the list, first (and above all) there is commitment and support by the highest levels of government that organizational change shall take place. Quite simply, the Chinese government has declared that various incentive approaches and economic organization more typical of capitalist countries will take place. Secondly, bureaucratic reformation is going on at an impressive rate. The bureaucratic changes that were made to allow international businesses to enter the special developmental zones outside of Hong Kong provide an example of how rapidly changes can be made to accommodate the investment concerns of foreign capital. India, a democracy, has no viable means of making similar changes.

Perhaps most impressively, the underlying uses of behavioral technology (group development, operant conditioning, participative decision making) are all realities in Chinese society. Unlike the rest of the Third World where the issue is how to train development agency managers to maximize behavioral technology and participation, the issue in China is how best to unleash these forces in the continued development of the country.

SUMMARY

In the development of Third World organizational change institutions, one is faced with a difficult, if not insurmountable, number of variables that have to be controlled.

On the one hand, there is the ultimate question of power and commitment at the national level to allow the changes that will make such organizations effective in their work with beneficiaries. Most governments are reactionary in the sense that they do not like to support efforts that allow greater control by beneficiaries or the development of community involvement.

Assuming, however, that the commitment is made, at the national level, to allow such fundamental changes to occur, one then has to deal with the issue of reforming the bureaucracies within the development organizations. The process of reforming people who have their own localized power base is one that typically meets resistance since change requires giving up their power and transferring it to the community and the people served by the organization. This, typically, is not done voluntarily and must receive a mandate from national authority. The people who carry out this role are rare and their skills too often diffused in the end. But they do exist, and as governments come to recognize the need for change to a more decentralized, participative developmental effort, the hope is that more of these people, suppressed at the moment, will be able to come forth and play a leadership role in the change process.

Once these two variables are controlled, there are many mechanisms that can come into play. The resources that international agencies can supply in the training of participative approaches have been described, and in an earlier chapter, it has been suggested that there is a supportive background of people who have been trained in such approaches through international education programs. The essential question for a number of countries is whether the primary variables of national commitment and bureaucratic reformation can be made. It is a question that too often is resolved by revolution. China followed the route of revolution and has succeeded in controlling the two major variables. Because of the nature of its culture and political system, China has also made significant advances in training organizations to utilize behavioral technology and participation. But the price has been high—over 50 years of conflict and millions of deaths. It is not a process that could be recommended to the rest of the Third World.

One would rather propose a route in which change can be made, but resolved by the will of the nation's people, as was recently done in the Philippines. The citizens decided that a new government commitment for greater involvement and bureaucratic reformation was necessary. They were able to do that with a minimum of bloodshed. The hope now is that the new Philippine government will get the international support it needs to carry out that change process and that it will have the time to train its developmental agencies in community involvement and participative approaches to development. If given time, that is the easiest task for the behavioral technology, as discussed in Chapter 2, already exists. The really difficult issues of political commitment and bureaucratic reform (at least in the Philippines) have to be resolved. Hopefully, five years from now, the Philippines will serve as a peaceful model, and provide the blueprint for how that process can be carried out, to all of the Third World.

Recognizing the difficulties in getting to the final step of training the people for indigenous Third World development organizations, the following chapter will outline some of the mechanisms that can be used in training staff members in participative approaches to organizational change.

NOTES

1. Morris J. Solomon and Flemming Heegard, "An Action-Training Strategy for Project Management," Development Project Management Center, International Training, ERS/FDD, U.S. Department of Agriculture, Washington, D.C., 1977, mimeographed.

2. Ibid.

3. Ibid.

4. Ibid.

5. Ibid.

6. Ibid.

7. Dave Korten and Felipe B. Alfonso, *Bureaucracy and the Poor* (New York: McGraw-Hill, 1981).

8. Allen Jedlicka, *Organization for Rural Development* (New York: Praeger, 1977).

9. From field notes during a West Africa field study, summer 1982.

10. Bruce Stakes, "Local Responses to Global Problems. A Key to Meeting Basic Human Needs." Worldwatch Paper A, Worldwatch Institute, Washington, D.C., February 1978.

11. David Korten, "The Management of Social Transformation," *Public Administration Review* (November/December 1981).

12. Stakes, "Local Responses."

6

Guidelines for Training Agents of Organizational Change

Just as Ernest Worthing [from *The Importance of Being Ernest*] began life in a handbag, so the gathering and hunting economy that gave issue to humankind was conceived in a carrier bag. Sharing and a highly developed sense of altruism followed naturally on. And so did leisure, and the first affluent society.

Richard Leakey
People of the Lake

INTRODUCTION

One of the concerns of this chapter will be to describe some of the behavioral training techniques that can be used to develop effective work groups. The emphasis is on using the power of the small group in the training process. But what one should also seriously consider is the nature of the sex of these working groups. As discussed in Chapter 2, there is reason to believe, not only from our ancient (very ancient) prehistory as well as from what we see today in the Third World family, that these teams should be female or dominated by females rather than the current overdomination of male leadership in Third World (or for that matter First World) change agencies--particularly in the use of group processes.

If we are to believe the evidence of how the human race evolved, going as far back as homo erectus, it was the technical invention (a women's invention) of the digging stick and carrier bag (to carry the roots and tubers she dug up) that ultimately led to civilization. From the time of homo erectus (and eventually homo sapiens), the female gave a substantive reason for social interaction and mutual economic behavior through group processes, an essential aspect of survival in hunting-gathering societies from which we have all come.

Leakey, by extending this argument and describing what might have taken place in homo erectus culture, further states that:

A crucial part of operating the mixed economy of gathering and hunting apart from the mediums of knowing where and when to find food, was the intensely enhanced social interaction particularly the psychological and emotional complexities of reciprocal altruism. Being part of a group co-operating in different ways to achieve the same goal can be a very frustrating business, as anyone who has ever served on a committee certainly knows. Restraint, persuasion, tact, submission, aggression, perception, and a good sense of humor, all play their part in successful cooperation.[1]

If we could return to those times, and do a bit of modern-day participant observation, we would probably find that it was the females who were creating these institutions, not the males. Similarly today, in the Third World, we find more often it is the women who take the major responsibility for insuring survival of the family. One further finds that when women work together in groups they typically do a far better job then men do for a variety of psychological and physiological reasons. The final section of this chapter, then, will briefly discuss why we should perhaps focus our organizational change efforts on female management. However, the sections before that final section will deal with guidelines on the types of training mechanisms that can be used for training both women and men to be effective team members and group decision makers.

One of the elements that must be recognized in the organizational change process is that an organization development specialist along with the technicians, administrators, beneficiaries, and so forth is a key element. In *Walden II*, this person would be the behavioral technologist--the person who would devise the specific training tools and modify them sufficiently so they matched the organizational environment of the particular organizational setting.

As with any change agent, it would be expected that this skill would be a temporary function organized with the specific intent that in the end the participants would take over the training function, and the specialist would remove himself so that no long-term dependency would be established. Change agents after all, by design, are supposed to leave once an organization has reached the state of maturity where they are no longer needed as an essential element. To be sure, there would be need of a backup consultant to learn new specific techniques, but with the specific intent that any backup consultant would be of a short-term nature.

The objective, in the end, of the kinds of training exercises to be presented in the following sections is to develop the agents who will carry out organizational changes and create the designs for the twenty-first century.

TYPOLOGIES AND FRAMEWORKS FOR TRAINING

An important reality in designing and training personnel for the new change organizations of the twenty-first century is that the uniqueness of each organizational setting will, to a large extent, dictate the final specific configuration of the change organization.

Social and behavioral scientists, in order to get their journeyman cards, have to follow the scientific method and be concerned about the replicability of the systems they develop. In work of this sort, that is a quest that can never really be satisfied, and one might add probably should not be attempted as existing resources already are too few and precious. The "concern is with developing frameworks for understanding the diagnosis of the system involved and the processes by which combinations appropriate to any given local setting can best be worked out."[2] That is the focus of this chapter, namely, to provide a framework by which an organizational change can be analyzed and training procedures selected (and modified to whatever cultural reality is necessary to make them relevant to the participant groups).

Moreover, in the context of developing countries, one must keep in mind the primary objective of organizational change, which is to improve the well-being of the people the change organization is to serve. In the introductory chapter it was stated that, if we are going to introduce organizational changes, we must also be concerned about the economic and technical components of the change process. Not only are we trying to improve the effectiveness of Third World change agents, but we are also trying to make a transition into a twenty-first century economic system that will be vastly different from what we have accepted as the conventional wisdom of the twentieth century.

In Chapter 1 it was suggested that a number of different developmental approaches that do not rely upon propping up the old, ineffectual subsistence approach will have to be developed if we are to look seriously at ways to resolve developmental problems. One of the first steps would be to agree upon what kind of technological alternatives might be applied for twenty-first century development and then begin the training for organizational changes that would promote that development. Consequently, the first step in the process of organizational change would be to formulate what developmental objectives the organization had in mind and its ultimate impact upon the beneficiary group it is intended to serve.

Before getting into the specific kinds of training techniques that could be used for making organizational changes, an outline or framework of a course of events that one would need to cover before initiating specific management training is provided. Such a framework of analysis might look like the following:

A Framework of Analysis to Change the Organization
to Better Serve the Primary Beneficiary Group

I. Establish Primary Objectives of the Organization

  A. Develop or acquire the kind of technology and development program that will benefit beneficiaries in the twenty-first century.

  B. Establish linkage with research and development institutes both outside and inside the country to determine what kind of technology will suit the twenty-first century.

  C. Establish assessment panels of the new technological alternatives and how they might be transferred to the beneficiaries.

    1. Select a panel composed of economists, technicians, organization administrators, extension personnel, organization development specialists, and beneficiaries.

    2. Determine what the key managerial problems are to carrying out the primary objectives of the organization.

    3. Determine what kind of training will be necessary to make organizatioal changes that will better serve the target beneficiaries.

The point of this divergence from the chapter's focus on the management and training of the change process is to remind the reader that effective management is not the whole issue. Obviously, the change organization has to have something to provide beneficiaries other than effective management alone. That something may be a new agricultural technology, a birth control program, or an educational program for beneficiaries. Whatever that program may be, as indicated in the previous outline, the organization will need to develop or acquire it, establish its linkage with research and development institutions, and assess the new technological alternatives and how they might be transferred. Once this latter plateau is reached, you return to the subject of the book, for effective transfer and evaluation rely upon effective management and the combined inputs of many different people in that assessment process. It is here where the training of these people play the essential role in selecting the technology or developing the program that will most effectively serve the beneficiaries.

COMMENTS ON THE TRAINING DIMENSION

At this point training would branch off from the technology assessment element of the change organization and focus on the specific kinds of management issues that would have to be addressed to produce an effective, beneficiary-oriented organizational approach. The development specialist, in consultation with other members, would assess what specific elements would have to be addressed. For example, if the organization were new (or was in the process of developing a new department) and had as a priority concern that all new members to be hired have a high degree of empathy with the beneficiary group as well as a high degree of willingness to work together in groups and promote participative decision-making techniques, there are a variety of psychological tests that can measure people on those dimensions. Those tests can be used as a screening device to select the desired people for the organization. Such a selection process was used in the Puebla Project discussed in Chapter 5.

Most commonly, however, the organization will have to deal with the people it already has. The issue then becomes identifying the key problem areas and determining what kind of training techniques can be used to resolve those problem areas. Problems that behavioral training could address include such areas as the degree of joint decision-making capability needed and how one could go about training people in such decision making. Members would need training in how to cooperate effectively with each other, how to resolve conflict between fellow workers and beneficiaries, and how to obtain field information through participant observation techniques. It all depends upon the internal and external environment of the organization.

Obviously, each organization has its own unique set of behavioral problems so that there can be no one right set of training procedures, but there can be one right set of attitudes toward the change process; namely, to be effective the organization has to include the beneficiaries in the change process and accordingly train its people to understand and be effective in promoting that process. Once that core belief is accepted, then the specific training exercises can be selected and used with organization members. While it is impossible to give examples of all possible problem areas and the kinds of training that could be provided to correct them in this chapter (the subject of training procedures is a book in itself), an example of a hypothetical organization, its major problems, and the kinds of training that could be utilized to correct those problems will be provided in the following sections.

ORGANIZATION X: AN ANALYSIS OF MAJOR PROBLEM AREAS

Upon analysis by a representative organizational team, including members of the beneficiary target group, and facilitated by an organization development specialist, the analysis team concluded that the major behavioral problems affecting organization X were the following:

1. There is a great deal of conflict in the organization, and people have difficulty working together. They need to learn how to resolve conflict and work together to be more effective in the field.

2. Potential team members have no real idea of how to go about implementing an effective joint decision-making effort. If team members are going to create organizational designs for the twenty-first century, which involves the contributions of beneficiaries, they must learn how to be effective in joint decision making.

3. Organization members behave in an insensitive manner both with themselves and with beneficiaries. This kind of conduct creates problems both within the organization and in fieldwork with beneficiaries. To improve the situation, a knowledge of positive reinforcement techniques would be useful.

4. Organization members do not understand how to get sufficient field information to use in the design of effective change programs. There is a need to teach them how to obtain such information.

5. As a subset of the information-gathering problem, it would be useful to know how to use the anthropologist's tool of participant observation to get an accurate profile of field problems. Training should also include how to go about using this kind of observation.

Of course, as has been repeatedly stated throughout the book, a top management commitment to analyzing and then resolving the organization's problems is essential. With that commitment, a specific package of training exercises can be developed and the training process begun.

In the following section, a series of exercises addressing the five problems above will be presented. The format of those exercises will be to state the problem area, provide the name of the exercises, supply a list of materials, state the objective of the exercise, and describe the procedure. The specific format will appear as illustrated below and will follow the consecutive order of the five problem areas listed above.

FORMAT
Problem Area.
Name of Training Exercise.
Materials.
Objectives.
Procedure.

With that format in mind, the following section will describe some specific training exercises that could be used to resolve the five problems brought out in the organizational problem analysis.

SPECIFIC TRAINING EXERCISES

Five consecutive training exercises will be presented that address the five consecutive problem areas defined in the previous section. The section begins with the description of a training exercise to resolve problem area 1.

Problem Area 1

Organization A experiences a great deal of conflict in its daily operations. Team members have to learn the importance of working together effectively.

Training Exercise Number 1. Working Together Effectively

Materials. One piece of watertight pipe (18 inches long), a ping-pong ball, a hammer, and one coathanger.

Objective. The primary objective is for team members to recognize that working together can be a highly effective process and can produce creative solutions to difficult problems. As a result of learning to work together effectively, it is hoped that group members will recognize the negative role that interpersonal conflict plays and begin to understand how they may go about reducing conflict between group members.

Procedure. Two things are important in the development of the problem-solving team. First, members of the team must understand that it is advantageous to cooperate in resolving problems. Second, members need to think of innovative solutions that do not follow standard conventional wisdom and that, in fact, may deviate considerably from standard behavior.

This training exercise was originally developed by another organization development specialist, but has been modified by the author for the Third World context.[3] Groups are brought to a room where a watertight pipe, approximately 18 inches long, is stuck upright on a concrete floor. Resting snugly in the bottom of the pipe is a ping-pong ball.

The group is given a hammer and a coathanger and told that their task is to get the ball out of the pipe without damaging it or scratching the pipe in any way. The usual response is to take the coathanger, flatten it with the hammer, and try to pop the ball out by sliding it between the side of the pipe and the ball. After considerable scratching of the pipe, groups using that approach find that it will not work.

It is a rare group that comes up with the correct solution, which is to urinate into the pipe and float the ball out. The earthiness of the solution is particularly appealing to rural development organizations.

What the exercise illustrates is that difficult problems require a different perspective for unique solutions. Such problem solving may require team members to deviate from standard behavior especially given the views that most cultures, and the cultural training they have had about what is acceptable behavior, have toward bodily functions such as urination. However, in creating twenty-first century organizational structures, that is precisely what will have to be done--one must deviate from standard behavior to create the new organizations. But above all, it illustrates the need for cooperation in developing solutions to problems. Without getting gross, one can imagine the kind of summations a trainer can make for this exercise.

Another point of the exercise is to show that technical solutions often have a behavioral component that far surpasses the technical and requires a unique way of thinking. This kind of thinking, because of the synergistic effect of group decision processes, is more likely to come from groups than from individuals.

One could manipulate the coathanger or pound the pipe all day to no effect. The point is that unique solutions to difficult problems, which will not respond to technology, are often based in human behavior. To create the designs for the twenty-first century, we will need to utilize the strengths that arise from participation, involvement, and group processes. Pounding the object of concern (a typical autocratic response) will not work.

Problem Area 2

Because potential team members have not received any previous training in joint decision making, it is difficult for teams to work together effectively. The basic training problem is compounded by the fact that some members are philosophically opposed to joint decision making and would rather make decisions on their own.

Training Exercise Number 2: How Individuals Can Become Effective Joint Decision Makers

Materials. Flip-chart paper, small workroom where people can be seated comfortably to promote a relaxed atmosphere.

Objectives. To explain the nature and importance of group decision making to group members who have not worked in such an environment. To illustrate the synergistic effect of people working together effectively in the small-group environment, and to teach some very specific group decision-making techniques such as nominal group theory and brainstorming.

Procedure. In joint decision making, the first step is to define the problem. A good format to use is two of the guidelines by Filly on how to define a problem:

1. Conduct a problem analysis to determine the basic issues. The concern here is to make sure that individual parties have not already developed their solutions. At this point, "it is essential to find out the specific needs or desires of the parties by asking them to define specifically what they wish to accomplish with their proposed solutions or objectives."[4] With facilitation by the organization development specialist, the group would then work to reach an understanding of the effect that predetermined solutions have on an interactive group process.

2. Identify obstacles to goal attainment.[5] If any members have a problem because of their cultural belief that beneficiaries are ignorant peasants who cannot play a meaningful role in developing solutions, then it is necessary to bring that out. If such members cannot modify their beliefs so that they can work effectively with the group (and it is not being argued that they actually

have to change their beliefs), then it will be necessary to remove them from the group. If deep-seated personal beliefs are involved, then it would take a great deal of personal counseling to change that belief (if it were even possible).

In the group solution process, there is of necessity both an individual and group process. Individuals are effective in generating ideas because they do not have to go through the interactive process of bouncing those ideas off of group members and coming to an agreement on which ideas should be tested. Groups, on the other hand, are more productive in evaluating plans that will result in a balance of ideas suitable to an acceptable solution for all parties because by definition they must be interactive, relying upon the specific opinion, discussion, and decision of all members of the group. Individuals certainly can be effective in evaluating ideas, but far too often one-sided, individual idea generation and evaluation result in a solution that is inappropriate to the needs of people the organization serves. Two techniques can be taught to group members to facilitate these processes: nominal group theory and brainstorming.

In the nominal group, after the problem is determined, group members are given a period of time (anywhere from 10 to 30 minutes) to list all the possible solutions. Then using a facilitator, group members read their solutions out loud starting with their first solution, which is recorded, and continuing until all have had a turn. The process is continued until all the members have read their solutions and a hierarchy of most important to least important solutions has been determined for each one.

The primary purpose of the nominal group approach is to allow for a rapid generation of ideas, which can be quickly obtained through individual effort. The obvious fault with the approach is that it does not allow for any interchange between individuals within the group because it is specifically structured so that verbal interplay cannot take place.

The writer prefers to modify the nominal group in a manner that purists would decry. In this modification, group participants begin the process in the traditional way of listing their solutions and developing hierarchies of solutions for each problem. Once that is completed, members are picked at random to present a rationale for their primary solution. Once the rationale has been explained, other members are allowed a period of time for free-field inquiries into the suitability of the solution and elaboration of parameters or constraints to the implementation of the solution. The solution, its rationale, and its constraints are written on flip-chart paper and posted on the wall. The same procedure is carried out with each member until all of the top-priority solutions have been analyzed by the group.

Once that step has been completed, the best solutions are selected. Ideas are randomly selected, and in a free-field discussion where all participants are equal in terms of their power relationships (beneficiaries as well as administrators), each solution is once again rigorously analyzed, developing more constraints to its implementation and rejecting the worst alternative until the three best solutions that the group agrees on remain. By this time one has probably reduced (for a seven-member group) some 35 individual, potential solutions to three ideas agreed upon by the groups, with an exhaustive list of potential parameters and constraints to implementing the ideas. That reduction represents the synergistic knowledge of all the group participants focusing their experience upon three potential solutions to an organizational problem. It is a process that requires a good degree of cooperation and tolerance for the conflict (as people give up ideas that are central to them) that of necessity must occur. Now the difficult part of the process begins.

To train people in the skills required to carry out this kind of group decision making, one needs to teach them how to control the conditions that lead to conflict in group processes, as a background skill to the total group decision-making effort. Once that background training has been accomplished, then the previously defined skills can be imprinted by having the organizational change team use a relatively minor in-house problem as the training vehicle, before they venture into the process of developing major organizational changes. Problem area 3 takes the reader one step further into the training process of integrating various group skills into a skilled team behavior and also illustrates how groups can study the effect of conflict and insensitivity upon the group and upon the effectiveness of the organization.

Problem Area 3

Organization members behave in an insensitive manner both with each other and with beneficiaries. This kind of conduct has created problems both within the organization and in fieldwork with beneficiaries. A knowledge of positive reinforcement techniques, it is believed, may improve organization member's communication with both themselves and with beneficiaries.

Training Exercise 3: Teaching Group Members to Positively Reinforce the Behavior of People They Work with

Materials. Flip-chart paper, a comfortable room, release time of several days to carry out the training.

Objectives. To teach participants the basic theory behind positive reinforcement, and to provide them the time to experiment with ways of positively reinforcing people in their respective job environments. It is expected that trainees will leave with a preliminary schedule of positive reinforcers to apply in their work environment.

Procedure. Group members are given a brief lecture describing the basic elements of positive reinforcement. That lecture emphasizes that all human behavior is directed toward goal accomplishment and that when a particular goal is accomplished and rewarded (by verbal reinforcement or any other means) a person will tend to repeat that behavior.

Group members are told that positive reinforcement has two objectives. The first is to enhance relationships within the organization between managers and employees. The second, and even more important, goal is to improve relationships between field representatives and beneficiaries. Positive experiences with democratic orientation and shared goal determination stand a better chance of success in the field (as has been stressed throughout this book) than indifferent or negatively reinforced interactions between organizational representatives and the people they serve.

Team members are told that positive reinforcement or operant conditioning is nothing new and that in fact many people figure it out for themselves or grow into it as they become older. The trick in organizational change is to train people who do not naturally have that skill, as quickly as possible. It can also be assumed that positive reinforcement is used in all cultures. The goals, however, may be different. For example, in Jivaro society in the old days, male children were operant conditioned to value the ritual of head hunting as a positive cultural value. Good socialist children in the Soviet Union get extra benefits for behaving in ways that are deemed good by the managers of that educational system, and black children in U.S. Head Start programs win tokens for behaving properly in learning their school lessons through a coordinated, positive reinforcement learning system. These are all examples of positive reinforcement that are used for different, but equally acceptable, objectives within different societies.

The Example of Jack—A Self-Made Operant Conditioner

Jack was a supervisor I worked under in a chemical plant where administrators were "distinguished" by autocratic behavior between administration and employees. Jack's management style was considerably deviant because he was friendly, concerned, and above all positively reinforcing in his dealing with subordinates. His style was to come to you, at different times during a work shift, and in addition to asking how things were going with you and your family, to use the occasion to compliment the good things you had done on the job.

In accordance with the theory, the reinforcement was not done continuously, but on a random basis, which, according to the theory, results in the strongest retention of a given behavior. At times, the reinforcement came when I was feeling somewhat depressed; so the special attention was particularly helpful. Jack's shift was the most productive in the plant, and in stark contrast to the other administrators, he was universally respected and admired throughout the plant.

But what must be mentioned is that Jack had never heard of operant conditioning or B. F. Skinner. At the time I had the pleasure of working for him, he was about 60 years old. He had learned this behavioral technology intuitively in the course of his tenure in the company and applied it effectively. Consequently, when we talk about the use of behavioral technology and operant conditioning in organizational designs for the twenty-first century, what we are looking for is either the selection of people like Jack (who by nature behave that way or have gained that skill through experience) or we have to train people to behave like Jack.

Method of Discussion

After an introduction to operant conditioning such as just explained, individual group members are asked to think back over the past five years and write down examples of when supervisors have verbally positively reinforced some behavior they manifested in their jobs. After listing each incident, they are asked to write down how they felt (or, in the case of illiterates, participants use the tape recorder).

The group then discusses the kinds of positive reinforcement they have received and their responses to them. A team recorder goes to the flip-chart, and the group searches for commonalities in their past experiences both in the kinds of verbal reinforcers that were used and in the responses to them. At this point a long break is taken. Members are required to take a walk and continue discussing the experiences they have had.

Upon returning from the group walk, members are assigned two tasks:

1. Develop a set of conditioners for use with the organization and project the responses they will receive from interorganization members. In addition, work out a schedule for using the reinforcers.
2. Develop a set of conditioners for use by field representatives with beneficiaries. Based upon the knowledge of cultural differences, once again project the kind of responses one might expect and develop a schedule using those reinforcers.

During this work session, which will extend for a period of a few days, the organization development trainer works with all groups in developing a reinforcement program. As stated in the beginning of this chapter, training exercises as much as possible are real-time experiences coming directly out of the organization's work environment instead of hypothetical exercises.

The Following Day

Groups report their conditioning programs to the whole group, and the other groups comment on their appropriateness, focusing on cultural and organizational relevance. All groups go through the same process. Then the entire training group develops a total group conditioning program for use within the organization, based upon the conditioners established by each group. A modified nominal group process as explained in the previous problem area description would be useful in selecting the specific conditioners.

A department from organization A is randomly picked, and the team members from the training program from that department are then requested to use the conditioning program in their department for two weeks. These people have already been taught in earlier training exercises how to record observations as participant observers (to be presented in problem area 5).

They report their experience to the whole group, both successes and failures, after the two-week pilot basis. In collaboration with top management officials (who of necessity have been members of the team-training effort), the rest of the training group experiments with operant conditioning in their respective departments. Over a six-month period, other administrators are brought into the training program, and the conditioners are modified based upon the field experience gained from initiating operant conditioning within the organization. Finally, the team is ready to work on developing an operant-conditioning system for work with beneficiaries in the field. The process used within the organization is also used with beneficiaries.

A Brief Digression

Returning to the original issue of how to bring about effective decision-making, the group will at some point need to acquire information that they can jointly use in making a decision. One way to obtain that information is through surveys of field respondents by group members. A way to analyze that information and use it for a basis of group decision-making is by utilizing the group technique defined in problem area 2.

A conventional condescending view is that people such as peasant farmers (team members) are not capable of doing an effective job. One argument is literacy; that is, if you are illiterate, first, you are not trainable, and second, since you cannot write, you cannot systematically keep records of what is taking place. The portable field tape recorder and videotape has negated that argument. Illiterate participants can easily use the tape recorder to get responses, and statisticians in the head office can tabulate the responses afterward. One should be able to imagine the power of having, for example, in an agricultural program, farmers (in organizational change teams) gathering data and suggestions for change from farmers. This is especially valuable if such a change agency has gone the extra distance and provides feedback to the farmers as the change process continues. A simple training procedure for nontechnical field researchers is provided in the following subsection. It can be used with tape recorders or hand-written responses to questions.

Problem Area 4

Team members have not been trained in techniques of obtaining field information that is useful to the development of effective change programs. Because accurate information is so relevant to the design of effective programs, it becomes necessary to provide trainees the means by which they can obtain information on their own.

Training Exercise Number 4: How to Learn Field Survey Techniques

Materials. Tape recorder, flip-chart paper, small room with movable chairs.

Objective. To illustrate the importance of gathering field information to be used in the design of innovative solutions for program development. The view is that both educated and relatively uneducated people can be effective field data gatherers. Specific training on how to gather data is provided. Team members are trained both in the use of tape recorders and hand-written methods as techniques of recording information.

Procedure. Members of the group are assembled with the organization development specialist, and team members are instructed about the importance of the interview in getting information to be used in designing organizational change. Role plays are used to get that part of the training across.

Using the tape recorder is a recommended procedure (particularly for novices, regardless of their education) since it takes some skill in getting novices to interview and record information simultaneously. Some people may suspect that people will not speak honestly into the microphone because of the fear that they will be punished later for what they said. That certainly could be true in an environment such as a U.S. university where administrators have an autocratic policy of punishing people for saying unkind things about their home institutions. It depends upon the nature of the questions. If respondents suspect that interviewers will use their responses against them at a future date, you will not get an accurate response even if a tape recorder is used. My experience in using tape-recorded interviews is that farmers were more than receptive to their use—particularly if they could hear the playback or be allowed to do other extemporaneous activities such as recording songs.

The Exercise. One team members plays the interviewee, and the other team member plays the interviewer. Seated facing each other with the other group members circled around the players (to analyze the session), the pair role play a field interview.

The specific context of the interview depends upon the nature of the organization that team members came from. If the organization is an agricultural development organization, the role play could be between an extension agent and a local farmer.

After the role play is finished, the observing group members report to the players how the interview came across. Specifically, the role players will be told whether they were too aggressive, violated local cultural practices, or failed to convey the required information.

All participants go through a role play as interviewers. At the end of the role play period, members compare their roles and comments and produce typologies of variables that promote or hinder interview effectiveness for the local cultural area.

These typologies will then be used in training exercise number 5, which is presented in the next section. While an actual field experience could be incorporated to imprint the training for problem area 4, the field experience is reserved for problem area 5.

Problem Area 5

Team members need a training in participant observation techniques in order to learn how to observe and record cultural behavior that relates to field problems for the development of an effective organizational structure to address those problems.

Training Exercise Number 5: How to Be an Effective Participant Observer

Materials. Flip-chart, chalkboard, movable chairs.

Objective. To illustrate to trainees the importance and technique of obtaining information while functioning as a member of an organization or culture. To learn how to acquire information from beneficiaries in the field that will lend further insight about designing programs that will help those beneficiaries. To show trainees that participant observation is a field survey technique.

Procedure. Trainees are given a presentation on the origins of participant observation from anthropological field research. It is important to show that, while informants can be expected to respond to questionnaire surveys and structured questions, even more important information can often be gained by observing people in the field. Recording that information for comparison with more formal information gathering helps in designing mechanisms that better serve organization beneficiaries. It is pointed out that at times people may behave in ways that can only be observed, and not obtained through a formal interview process. Such behavior, however, may be relevant to being able to work effectively with them. One example is the Bolivian Quechua who conduct a series of rituals before working in the fields. Participant observation of fieldwork discloses the importance of these rituals while a formal field interview might not even detect their existence, let alone importance. A good design, then, for work with such people would be to incorporate those rituals into the service organization's field activities with those clients.

Role Play. Several trainees carry out a prearranged skit of a hypothetical group of beneficiaries. The field-gathering trainers observe the skit and participate to the degree that the actors allow them to. They report their observations to the other trainees. To duplicate field conditions, trainees are asked to write down their observations. For those trainees who are illiterate, tape recorders are provided.

Real-Time Experience. Trainees, during the following week, are required to observe their coworkers in their respective departments and unobtrusively record any behaviors that may be unique or important to the successful function of their department. During the following training session, trainees report their observations and the relevance they have to their respective organization.

Field Experience. Following the organizational participant exercise, trainees are ready to test themselves in the field, using the cultural typologies of the beneficiaries they developed for problem area 4 in the previous section. Teams of participants are sent to local communities in the surrounding area with the task of finding out the single most important action that beneficiaries would like to see the team member's home organization carry out. Participants are observed by fellow team members as they carry out their interview procedures, and the interviewing trainees are evaluated for effectiveness in line with the typologies developed by the whole training group.

All teams return for a final session to compare their experiences. Trainers finish the exercise by reminding all group members of the importance of correct information in developing innovative organizational programs. In the course of that session, the trainer reminds the trainees that information that is insensitive to the cultural base of the beneficiaries will more likely be wrong and can result in the development of inadequate solutions to beneficiary problems.

The facilitator reemphasizes the fact that relevant information to successful organizational change is not always provided at discrete, convenient times. Like the anthropologist, the change agent is both a participant and observer and needs to be ready to observe and record any relevant information whenever it is available.

These are only a few of the exercises that could be used to address the five problem areas presented in the beginning of the chapter. Each exercise has been modified to match more closely a Third World work environment. These exercises by no means exhaust the available number that could be used. Hundreds exist and hundreds can be created or modified. And that has always been the point of this book, that the behavioral technology exists. But that as a handbook of universal solutions to all problems, for the specific environment of the organization will dictate the nature of the specific training exercises to be used to change the organization. The author has spent some 15 years developing these kinds of training programs and continues to work with a variety of international organizations. He knows firsthand both the difficulty of making such a change effort work and the satisfaction that comes when a program is successful.

The following section will address the first issue of this chapter, the role of women in organizational change, and will describe a training procedure to change organizational attitudes toward women.

WOMEN, TRAINING, AND CHANGE

As indicated in Chapter 2, it is believed that women have innate characteristics and behavioral realities that are different than men. Such attributes may, in fact, make women superior managers. Furthermore, in light of creating organizations that will change the world conditions in the twenty-first century, it is hoped that women will assume a pivotal role.

The majority of women everywhere are opposed to war, are dedicated to programs that foster the welfare of people in general regardless of one's own personal financial situation. They are deeply concerned with the plight of the poor, and with the environment. And most women, whether or not they have children, are committed to values favorable to the raising of children and to personal communal well-being.[6]

The view that women are superior is obviously one that is shared by few cultures, including the United States. Yet it is a reality that we should take advantage if we are serious about solving the major problems of development in the early twenty-first century. Women have been both a wasted and exploited resource in the twentieth century.

The role of women in international developmental agencies has, to some extent, been addressed (in part because in the United States a public law requires the role of women to be considered in international aid programs). Because of the effects of such international efforts as the 1975 U.N. World Women's Conference, men no longer attempt to transfer agricultural programs to men in countries where women control agriculture, as was routinely done in the 1950s and 1960s. However, the management capabilities of women are still either largely unknown, ignored, or repressed in most countries. It is believed that for change programs to be truly effective, an understanding of the role of women will have to be provided to all members of organizations involved in development.

The following training exercise gives some idea of how an organization could go about making its members aware of the management capabilities of women.

Problem Area 6

The home organization is characterized by an overwhelming perception that women are inferior to men both as managers and as keepers of the family in the beneficiary work area. A result is that the organization has been ineffective with work in the field because extension members refuse either to recognize the role of women or to work with them. Recently, top administrators, through the help of an outside consultant, have recognized the problem and have begun hiring more women. They decide to initiate a training program on the importance of women for all employers.

Training Exercise Number 6: The Receptivity of Female Managers to Organizational Change Efforts

Materials. Objective test on cultural stereotypes of women based upon the specific cultures of the country where training is taking place. Flip-chart paper for all work groups, room with movable chairs.

Objective. To illustrate to trainees that many myths associated with women are just that. Additionally, to show trainees that the very attributes one associates with women—nurturing, good communication skills, and the ability to follow through and to apply operant conditioning—are the very skills that are needed for effective implementation of organizational change in the twenty-first century.

Procedure 1. Team members take a test about stereotypes related to women (modified to match the culture of a specific country and region). Trainer then reads the correct responses to the group and asks members to discuss their answers for each question.

Members are then broken up into several work groups and requested to discuss questions that focus on how they can work with women and why women are, in fact, better administrators than men. The trainer works as a facilitator, making certain that participants do not avoid the specific issues, and keeps the discussion going.

After discussion, the trainer ends the session emphasizing that women play the essential role in development and that the team members will have to remember this as they design new organizational changes.

Procedure 2. Team members from the training effort, utilizing the participant observation technique they were taught earlier in the training program, will be required to visit selected homes of beneficiaries and live with the family for a week. During that time they will observe the family, and record, in particular, the management activities of the woman (or women) of the house, and make a report of everything that occurred during that week.

Team members must meet after the experience and compare their studies. A composite report representing the experience of the team is developed in preparation for a meeting of all teams. The modified group decision-making process, described earlier in the chapter, is used as the group decision-making tool in developing the composite report.

All teams meet and discuss their reports. The facilitator focuses teams on the significance of women's contributions to the management of the family and what that means in terms of designing programs to assist beneficiaries of the change organization.

SUMMARY OF TRAINING PROCEDURES

The preceding sections have shown how an organization could analyze its principal problem areas and develop a schedule of training exercises that would help change the behavior of organization members with respect to specific problem areas. It is a classic behavioral process for changing overt behavior without diving into deeper subconscious levels, as a psychoanalytical change process might do. As stated in Chapter 2, the advantage of such behavioral approaches is that they are relatively cheap, very fast, and usually quite effective.

There is, of course, a certain percentage of people who will not change regardless of what kind of effort is used. Change organization members who fall into this category will have to be replaced.

The training examples are not meant to be exhaustive (they hardly are), for each organizational environment is unique and will require its own set of training exercises to resolve its own particular problems. The role of the organizational development specialist, then, is particularly important, for it is the specialist, in combination with the help of all team members, who bears the primary responsibility for developing an effective training program.

One must not forget, however, the nonmanagement objectives (examples of which are provided in the first pages of this chapter). Specifically, if the management changes will not support the organization's overall objective of promoting specific technologies or programs and transferring them to beneficiaries, then there is little point in making these changes. This may appear obvious, but it serves as a warning for much too often in the past organizations have become so involved with the change process as an end in itself that they have neglected the purpose behind it. A suggestion is that, as the training proceeds, outside personnel (not specifically belonging to the training teams) be incorporated to remind the trainees of the ultimate purpose of the training and the primary objective, which is to promote the well-being of the beneficiaries.

The reader also needs to know that nothing that is presented here is particularly new and that many of the exercises presented above suffer from cultural bias, as discussed in Chapter 3. That is, while I have little doubt that these exercises would work with Mexican administrators and subsistence farmers (for in part I have used them in various training programs in that country), they probably would not work, in direct translation, with the Fulani tribe in eastern Nigeria. An assessment would have to be made, in such a case, of whether the exercises would translate effectively. Examples coming directly from the host culture would then have to be incorporated to maximize the effectiveness of the exercise. It is not a major undertaking provided there are people available who understand the need for such modifications and have the skill and understanding to do so.

The purpose of these training exercises is for the establishment of multicultural organizational development teams that could use analytical, group problem-solving tools, such as described in Chapter 2. The point that was made in Chapter 2 is that, without the proper integration of team members into a cohesive working unit that can successfully handle conflict and individual differences, the final product more likely will not properly serve the needs of beneficiaries. To that end, training of team members is essential in producing agents of organizational change for the twenty-first century.

FINAL COMMENTS

The behavioral technology for developing organizational change has been around for over 50 years. Unfortunately, it has not been used effectively as an agent for change in the past or for creating organizational designs for the twenty-first century. But what is positive is that we do have the tools to carry out the changes. We do not need a Manhattan project to develop behavioral technology. What we need is the commitment to carry that process out, not only in the Third World, but in the First, Second, and Fourth Worlds. What we need is world development.

Such a world development would not necessarily resemble a worldwide *Walden II,* although a worldwide commitment to condition our children to be less aggressive toward strangers or enemies probably would not hurt. There are societies that, to some extent, already do this. The Zuni Indians of northern New Mexico, for example, do make an effort to train their children to be less aggressive toward neighbors and strangers. Unfortunately, they are allowed to vent that aggression on nonhuman objects such as dogs and cats, so their operant conditioning techniques could be improved.

A worldwide state of peace and harmony is probably many years away, but in the transition we might be able to achieve a workable relationship. While it will not necessarily mean that we all love each other, we will at least know how to work with, understand, and accept the limitations of our differences. Greater participation at all levels in the organizations we belong to will promote that understanding. If there is one single key to creating the organizational designs of the twenty-first century, it is participation and involvement. Not surprisingly, this theme has been echoed throughout the book.

Throughout this book, the current dilemma of Third World development has been viewed from an organizational perspective. Specific management techniques that can be utilized in creating more effective organizations have been detailed. But in carrying out that process, the reader has been warned of the cultural bias one can encounter in initiating the change efforts. However, through the careful use of both beneficiaries and organization representatives in the design process, Third World organizational change mechanisms and the in-country institutions that can carry out that mission can either be modified or created anew. Finally, some very specific examples have been presented on how one goes about creating these innovative people—the agents of change who will create the organizational designs of the twenty-first century.

I end, however, my comments on the possibilities of actually creating these designs in much the same vein as I began in the first chapter. The path toward organizational righteousness is fraught with many dangers. The role and nature of government will greatly affect the way in which organizational change is promoted. Fortunately, as the century closes, we seem to have a window of opportunity in making significant changes because the members of autocratic, nondemocratically controlled Third World countries have been greatly reduced. Everywhere, democracy is raising its participative head in even such tightly controlled economies and social systems as China and the Soviet Union. At this writing, the Aquino government in the Philippines stands poised as a potentially outstanding example of how one could develop organizational designs for the twenty-first century.

The First World has a chance to complement this existing, liberated world situation. One hopes that it will rise to the occasion for, to supplement Third World change, the help of the First World is needed. To produce world development, it is essential that the behavior of the First World becomes integrated with the behavior of the Third World. Such a world development will be the subject of the last chapter.

NOTES

1. Richard Leakey, *People of the Lake: Mankind And Its Beginnings* (New York: Doubleday, 1978), p. 191.

2. David Korten, *Population And Social Development Management* (Institute de Estudies Superiores de Administracion: Caracas, Venezuela, 1979), p. 28.

3. James Adams, *Conceptual Blockbusting* (San Francisco: W. H. Freeman, 1974).

4. Alan C. Filly, *Interpersonal Conflict Resolution* (Glenview, Ill.: Scott, Foresman, 1975), p. 112.

5. Ibid.

6. Marilyn French, *Beyond Power* (New York: Summit Books, 1985).

7

Toward a World Development

What is the original nature of man? I mean, what are the basic psychological characteristics of human behavior—the inherited characteristics, if any, and the possibilities of modifying them and creating others? That's certainly an experimental question—for a science of behavior to answer. And what are the techniques, the engineering practices, which will shape the behavior of the members of a group so that they will function smoothly for the benefit of all? That's also an experimental question, Mr. Castle—to be answered by a behavioral technology. It requires all of the techniques of applied psychology. From the precious ways of keeping in touch with opinions and attitudes to the educational and persuasive practices which shape the individual from the cubicle to the grave. Experimentation, Mr. Castle, not reason. Experimentation with life—could *anything be more fascinating?*

B. F. Skinner
Walden II

INTRODUCTION

The principal thesis of this book has been that properly managed organizational change efforts (along with the specialized training of target personnel and beneficiaries) will lead to better development of Third World countries and that we can, in fact, build designs for the twenty-first century that will improve the human condition.

That process, which has been described throughout the book, will not be an easy one. It is fraught with elements and variables that are difficult to control if, in fact, they are controllable. Some of those variables include the nature of the political system, the willingness of top officials to make a commitment to change, and the limitations of in-country staff to carry out that task once the commitment has been made.

Once a commitment is made, however, whether from scavenging one's in-country's training sources, participating with the international organizations of developed countries, or temporarily hiring expatriates, the talent is available to do the job, provided leadership to use that talent also exists. Several examples of the role of leadership have been provided in earlier chapters.

A predominant theme in developing designs for the twenty-first century is the role of participation and group processes in carrying out change, for the reality is that isolated technicians cannot understand the complexity of change without input from the field. They make stupid mistakes and, without training in ways to incorporate beneficiaries and their field knowledge into the decision-making process, will continue to make stupid mistakes. Alvin Toffler addresses that reality squarely in stating that

highly intelligent men and women are making stupider and stupider decisions—in politics, in industry . . . in every field. The quality of our decision-making is deteriorating across the board. Not because the people in charge are stupid but because they are making too many decisions too fast about things they know too little about.[1]

The solution to this dilemma is to allow more participatory management involving workers or beneficiaries to participate in the process and provide top-level decision makers with the information they need to make correct decisions. Without that right to participate, one cannot expect accurate information to be relayed to upper levels. There is little incentive to do that if you are merely an information conduit rather than a part of the final process. That issue is as real for the First World as it is for the Third. Toffler states, correctly, that he does not "mean to suggest that all this [participative structures] happens without conflict.[2]

Similarly for the Third World, he is correct in his view of worldwide participation that, "in societies still heavily impregnated with racism, sexism, disadvantaged groups will have to fight for every opening in the decision-structure."[3] They fought successfully in China with an expensive payment in lives, and they fought successfully in the Philippines with a minimum expense of lives, and we can only wish for the long-term success of that latter revolution—hopefully it will succeed and serve as the model for the twenty-first century.

But that is a transformation process, and such processes have costs.

To transform successfully companies or industries [as well as Third World change organizations] they have to do a lot of other things as well. They have to restructure themselves organizationally. They have to learn to trust their employees [and beneficiaries] as individuals. They have to customize their products and distribution . . . they have to move to smaller units, to more employee participation. For the twenty-first century, training will become a major industry. Not training just for specific job skills, but for something we don't know how to do very well. Helping people transition to wholly new ways of life.[4]

The argument made, throughout the text, is that to create effective Third World development, personnel in the change organizations must also become creative social, political, and humanistic change agents.

While all of this may lead to a new world order, the techniques by which that can be achieved come out of the late industrial revolution (admittedly by reformers). According to Toffler, the late industrial revolution revealed the first fleeting cracks in the power system, when

demands for participation in management, for shared decision-making, for worker, consumer, and citizen control and for anticipatory democracy came in nation after nation. New ways of organizing along less hierarchical and more ad-hocratic lines are springing up in the most advanced industries. Pressures for decentralization of power intensify. And managers become more and more dependent upon information from below.[5]

The point has been made that the techniques to create these participative skills already exist, and some of those techniques were detailed in Chapter 6.

Those participative skills will be needed by all administrators and all societies for the primary task of the twenty-first century will be to integrate all of today's differentiated societies into a truly world community. Despite our current problems of international terrorism and the chance of nuclear Armageddon, the unmistakable signs of a unifying world behavior are there. Behavioral technology is being used for both good and evil. The terrorists, after all, use Western techniques (along with extreme cruelty) to get their message across—news reports, war protests, and the operant conditioning of prisoners. Mikhail Gorbachev, in his increasingly conciliatory interaction with the West, is motivated by his fellow citizens' drive for better consumer products and less heavy industry. His means again match those of the West—news media, requests for a more humanistic style of interaction with his opponents, and an emphasis on more decentralization (along with accountability) in the Soviet economic system. And whenever one moves toward decentralization, the chance of developing a more democratic environment is increased, for decentralization requires one to go beyond behavior that follows a party line and to accept responsibility.

In organizational change and management training, the process is not restricted just to the members of the change agencies within Third World countries, but of necessity includes the beneficiaries. In other words, beneficiaries of change systems will also have to be trained in the fundamentals of participatory decision making, of group problem solving. They will need training to become effective research adjuncts to specialized scientists for, unfortunately, such behavior is not, at this point, a natural behavior of most beneficiaries for whatever historical or cultural reasons. Fortunately, the examples of Bolivian and Mexican farmers illustrate (in the areas of initiating risk-taking behavior in group decision making) that it is not very difficult to train such people to become effective group decision makers—provided the technical liaison and service exists to supply that training as well as the integration into change agency activities.

Again the argument of Bennis must be recognized.[6] Participatory decision-making will produce conflict because it cannot be controlled as a centralized decision-making structure can be. Consequently, the central organization will need administrators who can be selected and trained for their ability to handle decentralized, humanistic operations when beneficiaries are treated as equals.[7] In the change agencies of the immediate future, it is also possible to conceive of the use of relatively instant communication from trained work groups in the field. This could be in the form of a village computer with two-way radio systems powered by solar generators. We no longer have to think about the huge investment of utility grids to service rural communities in the next century. Low-cost photovoltaic systems already exist to power low-wattage communication and computer systems, and amorphous crystalization will provide household electricity early in the twenty-first century.

Once you have trained your organization in how to decentralize conflict resolution and how to use village decision-making processes, you can reduce your extension case load (on the assumption that training in the change agency's facility has been done adequately) through use of participative management systems.

The beauty about this scenario is that all the elements are there. All we need is the commitment to apply those elements into organizational change efforts. That simple parameter means we are almost there—or will never be there. One must hope that such a commitment will be there for the twenty-first century.

THE PRESENT STATE OF THIRD WORLD DEVELOPMENT—A WINDOW OF OPPORTUNITY?

In terms of total world development, the situation, despite the current drought in the Sahel, looks more optimistic than it did ten years ago. In fact, a USDA report concerning the current problems will continue as a result of the elimination of farm subsidies, due to the ability of the developing countries to significantly increase agricultural production through low-technology methods. The successful application of technology has brought economic terror to the U.S. farmer. Exports are down.

Looking at agriculture production on a worldwide basis, China has increased its production 50 percent largely through the peasant incentive system it initiated (again more participation in the development process) in the early 1980s. Malaysia is growing and exporting more rice than the United States. Brazil has become a major competitor in soybeans. The picture for the rest of the Third World is less rosy, but with the exception of Africa, we will probably not see any mass starvation into the twenty-first century. However, chronic malnutrition and protein deficiency will probably increase as populations continue to expand.

Dietary realities have also changed the patterns of agriculture. That one-pound steak that requires an 8:1 feed ratio to produce (in contrast to chicken, turkey, rabbits, and fish, which have feed ratios ranging from 3:1 to 1:1) has been found to be unhealthy, and dicts have accordingly been modified. In the future, there will not be a need to waste hundreds of thousands of acres on feed grains for inefficient meat production. With an appropriate (small) addition of meat, vegetables, and an all-purpose vitamin pill, a subsistence diet is a better diet than a developed country diet. New innovations such as perennial corn and nitrogen fixation wheat will make continued advances in the Third World (as much as they will dislocate farmers in the developed world).

But the significance, possibly, of focusing upon organizational change through agriculture and rural development agencies is that during this final transition the participatory skills that beneficiaries learn by working in agricultural reformation can be used in developing other economic sectors. The focus of organizational change, then, will be in devising ways by which people can obtain a larger share of the good life rather than barely holding on to the subsistence life.

The correct avenue of development has always been through agriculture and rural development for once people are being fed on a consistent basis one can start looking at other needs to fulfill. Despite the limitation of Maslow's theory of need satisfaction, one thing is certain. The first need, physiological need satisfaction, is paramount. People gotta eat.

If we wish to accept these somewhat rosy projections (they are, however, questionable) of food production for the next 20 years, then maybe a miracle is occurring. Perhaps we are, in fact, going to be given a "window of opportunity" to put a cap on development and organizational change in the Third World. It could be done in 20 years, and possibly we are being given that chance. Organizational change throughout the world, a truly world development, could greatly accelerate and increase the impact of that process.

But even as I write this, Ethiopia is expanding its efforts to collectivize its farmlands into a system not unlike the Ujamaa system detailed in Chapter 3. The predictable result is that thousands of Ethiopians are fleeing the country (some 50,000 at this writing) to neighboring Somalia. Since these farmers are among the most productive in Ethiopia (members of the Oromo tribes), two unnecessary results are occurring: Ethiopia, now that it has its rain, is losing its best food producers, and Somalia (which cannot afford it) has inherited a major refugee problem that it is finding very difficult to control.[8]

It is ironic that at the time the major socialist countries, the Soviet Union and China, have recognized that collectivized agriculture does not work (in addition to all the other failures of collectivized agriculture in Africa) the citizens of Ethiopia are compelled to participate in what can safely be predicted to be a disastrous agriculture program. Given the instability of the region, however, one can predict that there is a good likelihood that the present government will not be around long enough to do permanent damage.

In general, however, the trend is toward an individualized, participative agricultural expansion (despite such anomalies as Ethiopia), and a focus on world development will aid that process. The final section of this chapter will discuss ways by which we might achieve a world development as the ultimate design of the twenty-first century.

TOWARD A WORLD DEVELOPMENT

The focus of this book has been an organizational change in the Third World stressing the need to create designs that will improve the human condition worldwide in the early twenty-first century. It is a massive job, despite occasional glimmers of hope (or the windows of opportunities we may perceive). The simple reality is that somewhere around 2020 world population will soar from roughly 4.5 billion to 9 billion (give or take a few million). That means, somehow, the world in 30 years will have to double its present production capacity in everything just to maintain the world in its present situation (where roughly 60 percent of the population is chronically malnourished or worse). There is no vision of a VCR and a Toyota in every home throughout the world. Hopefully, there will be at least some rice.

It is not exactly a new proposition that the living standards of the First World has something to do with all this. Our demand for exotic materials is often supplied by the ill-paid labors of the Third World people. Our consumption of nonrenewable resources such as oil may mean that the Third World countries that now supply those resources will probably never enjoy them in the same consuming manner (as we have for the past 30 years) regardless of what future conservation measures we take. And the reluctance of the First World to help the Third World will gain us a place in history as a body of primarily Christian nations that did not behave like Christians. Europe has been a bit better than the United States in aiding the Third World (the former has given an average of almost 3 percent of its GNP for aid to development, while the United States contributes about 1 percent). We could rationalize that, saying it is the duty of European nations in the first place, returning some of what they took during the colonial period. Overall, such contributions are negligible, and the Group of 77, when it rants in the United Nations about neocolonialism and technical domination, is basically right. We, the First World, still control the world economy, and we are not about to give it up.

If it is any consolation, the only real problem here, if we look at the basic nature of human behavior, is that one group resents the control of the other. It just so happens, at this particular time in history, that those in power happen to have white-colored skins. When the Arab nations dominated the world economy prior to the Renaissance in Europe, one has no records that Arab agents of change went forth to help the peoples of Central Europe who were in a backward state of development. They did, however, try to conquer them and retained their colonial foothold in Europe well into the seventeenth century. What is the difference between fifteenth century and twentieth century exploitation— primarily the degree of brutality more common in earlier centuries. The real issue is that dark-skinned people, in the past, behaved no differently than white-skinned people do now. For a modern example, look at the Arab oil nations. Prior to the discovery of oil in the 1950s, the area was dirt poor. It no longer is, but does one see any outpouring of concern and outlay of funds by the Arab nations to help develop the less affluent Third World countries? Damn little unless there is a political motive to prop up a country that serves its interests. But does one see the Group 77 condemning the Arab nations in the U.N. General Assembly—not really.

All of these arguments do not mean that the First World does not have to feel guilty about its lack of concern for the rest of the world. It merely indicates that we are not acting inhuman. In fact, we are acting quite human. But it is time to change that. If the future generations of First World countries want a monument to their place in history, it should be dedicated to their attempt to create a truly world development. Three ways of accomplishing that objective come to mind: the use of operant conditioning as an adjunct tool in organizational change throughout the world; the increasing involvement of women at all levels in that change process; and the implementation of a "value-added" world tax on First World citizens.

OPERANT CONDITIONING AND WORLD DEVELOPMENT

The United States is currently undergoing a soul-wrenching analysis of the status of its educational system. We are finally admitting that many problems exist in the public schools. We have long known, at least the professors, but not the administrators (who are not particularly concerned about the quality of education), that the majority of the universities are doing a terrible job, producing a badly educated product and allowing too many students to enter nonproductive areas of education such as business. So far there has been a great deal of talk and limited action, but there is a vast potential to create the environment that will lead to world development through the educational system—by the conditioning of children. Again, it is not something that is evil, as so many still want to ascribe to the mild-mannered suggestions of *Walden II*. It is something that has already been done, at least on pilot scale versions.

In the late 1940s and early 1950s, the California educational system experimented with what was called progressive education. At the time, this was viewed as revolutionary for its underlying philosophy (in the elementary grades) was that the teacher was a nurturer, a coach, and not an autocratic disciplinarian. Operant conditioning in the form of special rewards (release time reward, for example, to work on one's individual project when the student had completed the basic classwork) was an integrated part of the curriculum. The world understanding component in the elementary grades was particularly outstanding. As part of the educational process, students were trained both in manual and academic skills. Classrooms were also workrooms equipped with lumber, carpentry tools, and art equipment. Each year students had a specific culture to study along with a related manual project. For example, when students studied the Hopi culture for one semester, they would also build a "Hopi village" in the classroom. Another semester might be the study of Mexican culture and the building of a Mexican "home" and utensils that the inhabitants used. The result was that the students not only studied different cultures, but in a sense also lived them.

Certainly the process can be very effective. I speak with some knowledge, having been an elementary student in California from 1947 to 1953. I can still clearly remember the fourth grade cultural project of study on Bolivian culture and building a "Bolivian" house. I am fairly certain that early experience had some effect in my later joining the Peace Corps and selecting Bolivia as my host country. Other Californians of the same era have reported the same feelings about the progressive education system.

Parallel to the objectives of *Walden II,* we can shape the behavior of our young people to be more understanding of different cultures through operant conditioning. After all it has been done on a pilot basis in California and undoubtedly is done on an ad-hoc basis in other school systems.

There are some promising events that may indicate that a change in thinking from the "me only" attitude of the yuppies to a world concern is beginning to develop. The recent Soviet-U.S. children's debates broadcast via satellite show that many of our children are at least not viewing the Soviets as uniformally evil, monolithic communists. The recent Hands Across America may be an indicator of increasing concern for less fortunate U.S. citizens, and the recent fifteenfold increase in Peace Corps applications (in contrast to the late 1970s when the Peace Corps could barely fill half of its quota of volunteers) could be taken as an increase in international awareness on the part of university students.

The point is that there is much that could be done through our educational systems to shape our future generations to be understanding and supportive of world development. Such a shaping would not be brainwashing or a drift toward totalitarianism, but more a focus that could morally help not only this country and other First World countries, but also be the means by which world development could be internalized as a universal objective of all educated people. Hopefully, as we as a nation resolve our current educational quagmire, some sense of world responsibility will become a conditioned part of all public educational systems.

WOMEN AND WORLD DEVELOPMENT

A previously stated proposition has been that women are better suited than men to develop and manage participative organizational structures. By nature, women are better at the nurturing and humanistic aspects of interpersonal relationships in participative management structures then are men. Also by nature their skills in developing and managing small-group processes are superior. It would seem rational, in creating the designs for the twenty-first century, that women should play an increasingly important role in that process.

It remains to be seen whether men will allow that to happen for in many countries that has been a major change process that in itself has caused some conflict. Supposedly, there is a whole range of mildly neurotic diseases that affect certain U.S. men as their wives assert their independence and make greater demands, upon their husbands, for equal rights. As this trend continues, it is already becoming obvious that the pattern of male/female relationships will be changed dramatically in the twenty-first century. Given the administrative capabilities of women, and the historical failings of men described in Chapter 2, one would assume that such a change would be for the better.

Given the increasing strength of women's movements throughout First World countries, it is difficult to imagine that behavior in those countries will return to that of the "Beaver's" mother or the "Stepford Wives" or even of the days of the Free Speech Movement (FSM). In the last case, women stormed the terraced steps of the Berkeley administrative buildings alongside their male comrades whose leaders, despite the egalitarian dogma of the movement, felt that women's best position in the movement was on their backs. First World women have already been liberated and are in the process of consolidating their power. Given all the inherent advantages that women have both in administration and concern for a world that is less hostile and more egalitarian, we should welcome and encourage their leadership in world development.

THE "VALUE-ADDED" WORLD TAX AND VOLUNTARY DEVELOPMENT AGENCIES

A final concern of world development is the means of financing the effort. First World countries could take the leadership by imposing a "value-added" tax on certain products such as cigarettes and liquor. With regard to the cigarette industry in the United States alone (roughly $5 billion in sales a year), a world development tax of 1 percent would generate $500 million a year and increase the price of cigarettes about 2 cents a pack. Impose the same tax on liquor, cosmetics, and second homes (the milieu of the affluent), and one could generate several billion dollars a year at insignificant increases in consumer price.

Extend that tax to all First World countries, and one could quickly generate an income of about $25 billion a year—a sizable treasury to work from.

The administration of such funds, for both Third World and worldwide development, would have to be accomplished by voluntary organizations. Unfortunately, no government agency could handle such a program without distorting the distribution process to serve political ends or without creating an inefficient bureaucratic structure that would waste much of the money just in paying for its operations. Organizations such as CARE and the United Way—which cut their overhead to the bone—could serve as a model for developing the organizational structure. A role for volunteers who are retired would be an integral part of the system. There are thousands of people, former managers, engineers, professors, who could work as administrators, trainers, and project developers. Many already do in organizations such as Volunteers for Technical Assistance (VITA). Person-power would not be a problem.

The efforts of such organizations would be truly international both in management and site development—they would not be restricted to the Third World. For example, it is conceivable that a project to develop a computer training program for displaced farmers in the northeast region of Iowa (now subsisting on food stamps and Aid to Dependent Children money) could be developed by a team composed of Russians, Zulus, Japanese, and Iranians. While a team of Iowans (from a more fortunate region of the state) together with Dutch Malaysian farmers could develop an agricultural project for Sahelian farmers in Chad.

For Third World development, one must abandon the idea that only the First World countries have something to contribute in the revolution of developmental problems. Teams and funding will be international. The means by which those teams can be trained to function effectively have been presented in earlier chapters. With all the prototype organizations such as VITA to serve as models, such an approach to world development could become a major vehicle for world development in the early twenty-first century.

SUMMARY

The twenty-first century may provide a window for effective world development. Despite the current problems of terrorism and assorted small wars, there is more communication about the need to change the world condition than ever before. In the United States, there seems to be a change of attitude in university students to more concern for the world condition and our immediate futures. Modifications in our educational systems, using behavioral tools such as operant conditioning, can expand this concern in our citizenry, as well as imprint an ability for people to serve in participative, small-group–directed change efforts. Women, retired people, "value-added" tax systems, and voluntary organizations could further complement and promote the effectiveness of world development for, as earlier chapters in this book have shown, the behavioral technology to carry out the training process has long existed.

A WORLD ORGANIZATIONAL CHANGE EFFORT

Given that our children are taught the values of world development, that we all accept the important role women play in participative organizational structures, and that change is financed through a world value-added tax, we are in a position to make a major world organizational change effort.

With the new communications systems, it is not inconceivable to have multidisciplinary teams composed of Russians, Americans, Argentinians, and Zulus plugged into low-earth orbit satellite systems—instantly discussing the design of an organizational system as though they were living across town from each other. The necessary commonality is that all participants would understand and accept the ground rules for participative management, group development, and small-group, decision-making processes.

A prototype of a world design system is currently being developed at the University of Northern Iowa (UNI) between faculty and students of UNI and Chinese university counterparts.[9] In this system, counterparts in both universities will be trained in participative structures, organizational design, project management, and communication satellite systems. The first objective is carrying out a consistent training program.

This book has already illustrated the advantages the Chinese have in using operant conditioning as an organizational change tool. It is anticipated that the UNI faculty and students would learn much from their Chinese counterparts on how to utilize the technique in organizational change. The U.S. participants would offer their experience in participative management, organizational design, and linkage with national and international information sources. The result would be a marriage of both of the participants' strengths in a form that cannot be precisely described until it is finally developed. What can be said now is that it will be a world approach to organizational change and development that will represent a prototype of an internationally integrated world development process that one would expect to become commonplace in the twenty-first century.

Another world development mechanism, using both the power of international work teams (united in their philosophy) and the ultimate responsibility of international corporations (their stockholders), is already being tested in a prototype form with companies in South Africa. It is stockholders who are pressing their company boards to get out of South Africa. It has not been a management choice, but like good managers, they ultimately follow the dictates of their stockholders.

In Chapter 4, an effort was made to show what international companies are doing to promote world development—not much. But it was also shown that those companies are effective managers and figure out ways to make a buck subject to the environmental constraints they face. In the twenty-first century, the new environmental constraint they will face is tighter control by "world" directed stockholders.

For example, the world design teams already discussed could organize purchases of selected company stock and, once a majority is attained, vote in a bloc to determine company policy. This could be a stronger controlling device than the set of laws of any single host country for it could not be corrupted by the countervailing activities of a particular company. With such majority-controlled bodies, a number of policies could be imposed that could still allow the company to make a profit. A certain percentage of profits could be required to be invested into infrastructure development that would benefit the host country (not the foreign company) or be invested in research and development for indigenous products that may ultimately have a world market, as well as improve the salaries of indigenous people. In some cases, salary increases are actually painless. Take the example of the U.S. company in Juarez, Mexico, that pays one-half cent in labor for each shoe its Mexican laborers produce. To double the labor price to a penny a shoe would increase the workers' salary from $4 a day to $8 a day.[10]

Yet on its own, the company will not take the plunge and increase its manufacturing cost one-half cent. A proper stockholder control could require that change. There are many examples of how such painless changes could promote world development, but currently are not being put into practice. One can also hope that, as this process is carried out, the business schools will have changed their curriculum to produce a product that will complement the activities of such world stockholder organizations. The implication for world organizational change just from this modification in education is quite significant. The people predominately trained in organizational change and design mostly come out of the business schools. Given the nature of business, if we can alter the nature of the people who run business to that of a concern for world development, the potential for change is much greater than all the world's international development agencies.

FINAL COMMENTS

This final chapter has been written to suggest to the reader that not only is there a Third World development problem, but also a world development problem. The task for the twenty-first century is to make the organizational changes, on a worldwide basis, that will integrate the Third World with the First World. The creation of a new international economic order that will emphasize participation, democracy, and involvement of all the world's people is mandatory. Satellite systems and continued breakthroughs in instant translation computers will make that economically viable within ten years.

There is much that can be done to improve Third World development and establish the groundwork for an integrated world development. Organizational change and the techniques promoting that process can and should play a role. While we most likely will never achieve the state of a *Walden II* where everybody functions for the benefit of all (certainly the Soviet Union has shown us that socialist paradises on earth are difficult to achieve), we can certainly do better than we presently are without destroying the Western sense of individuality.

A democratic world development recognizes that there will always be conflict but also recognizes that through participation, design involvement, and training those conflicts can be resolved. But for Third World and worldwide development, our designs for the future will always have to account and control for the human reality of conflict.

It has been fashionable to end behavioral-based books with some comment on the nature of man. A common ending has been to say something about the innate viciousness of human behavior, à la *The Naked Ape,* expressing the view that our basically Cro-Magnon bodies control our hormones and intolerant behavior of others.

But recent archaeological evidence and studies of the few surviving hunting-gathering societies show a past that is considerably different. Such a past is more consistent with *Walden II* where, in fact, the behavior of group members was shaped so they would function smoothly for the benefit of all. It was civilization that changed that behavioral process and introduced the excesses in contemporary male-dominated societies—war, exploitation of man, domination of women, and a general insensitivity to others. In our approximately 4 million-year evolution, it has been only the past 10,000 years in which basic human values have been distorted to the inhuman values predominant today. It is only 13 years until we start the next 10,000 years, and there is really no reason why we cannot begin changing our behavior to what it was originally. After all if Cro-Magnon and homo erectus populations could use a behavioral technology to turn their group members into people who worked for the benefit of all, surely the most technically competent civilizations can do likewise. As the preceding chapters have shown, the behavioral technology exists, and women will probably become the key leaders in its implementation.

The twenty-first century will be the time for creating world development, which will require substantive behavioral changes from the status quo of today's predominantly nineteenth century organizational behavior. But it is a process that should not be viewed as threatening, for we have the means to carry out those changes. The twenty-first century will become the time when the Third World will become part of the First World, and we no longer will think in terms of the different worlds that we do today. As we continue to develop that path of world development, organizational change and behavioral technology will play a substantial role in creating the designs of the twenty-first century.

NOTES

1. Alvin Toffler, *Previews and Premises* (New York: William Morrow, 1983), p. 106.
2. Ibid., p. 107.
3. Ibid., p. 108.
4. Ibid., p. 183.
5. Ibid., p. 163.
6. Warren Bennis, *Changing Organizations* (New York: McGraw-Hill, 1966).
7. Abraham Maslow, *Eupsychian Management: A Journal* (Homewood, Ill.: Irwin-Dorsey, 1965).
8. P. Revzin, "African Migration," *Wall Street Journal*, May 27, 1986, p. 2.
9. Allen Jedlicka, "An Appropriate Technology Transfer," *Interciencia* 10 (September-October, 1985), p. 45.
10. G. Erb, "Jobs Migration," *Des Moines Register*, March 24, 1986.

Index

About the Author

Allen Jedlicka is Professor of International Business and Organizational Behavior, and Coordinator of International Business Programs at the School of Business, University of Northern Iowa. He has spent twenty years researching organizational change in Third World countries and is the author of *Organization for Rural Development: Risk Taking and Appropriate Technology,* also published by Praeger.